Southern Independence.

Why War?

SOUTHERN INDEPENDENCE. WHY WAR?

THE WAR TO PREVENT SOUTHERN INDEPENDENCE

PRODUCED IN THE REPUBLIC OF SOUTH CAROLINA BY

SHOTWELL PUBLISHING LLC
POST OFFICE BOX 2592
COLUMBIA, SO. CAROLINA 29202

ShotwellPublishing.com

ISBN-13: 978-0692713778
ISBN- 0692713778

10 9 8 7 6 5 4 3

Hard as it is for a Yankee to understand or a Jacobin to admit, the fact is that the South had a harmonious and happy society, healthy from mutual dependence and common feeling: far more integrated than today or ever will be again. White and black worked together in the fields. Their children played between the rows, or carried plants. Not yet come was the divide-and-conquer strategy of the compassionate politicians and lawyers making hate to extort power and create "victim" and "villain" to extort money.

Once or twice a month, some older colored woman (e.g. Daisy Mayo, Cora Montgomery, Essie Streeter, and Oreba Person) tells me: "When we were young everybody, white and colored, helped one another. The spirit then was love." Is that the testimony of people estranged?

There was no pay for not working, so everybody had a job. Yet to come were the army of government agents, patronage recipients, administrators, holding no job jobs, invading and interfering with productive industry by accusing their operators of crimes invented for that purpose. The woods were not full of ambitious trolls, warlocks, and pismires seeking power by stirring discord. The hate-stirrers were not yet stirring. That deliberate operation to make hate lay quiet until after World War II.

Virtue was rewarded, vice punished. That practice was better for character and society. People liked one another. That was the basis of behavior. Everybody knew the Gospel of Love as standard. They may have not reached it but they were based on it, oriented by it. They feared more the consequences of sin than the mere punishments of law. They feared their parents; they feared society's censure.

If a colored person committed a crime his neighbors would call the police and he would be arrested as soon as he got home. School teachers and police paddled bad boys, often at the request of their parents. It was a safe place and a wholesome place, and a mannerly place. Everybody said, "Yes Sir," and "Yes Ma'am." Richard Weaver said the South was the last non-materialist society in the Western World. Observers have called the South the only civilization where all classes of society subscribed to the values of the aristocrats. Europeans said of the United States: "In the North they live for getting and having. In the South they live for being." Nelson Hopkins said, "There ain't but one thing north of Potomac River worth having. A one-way ticket back South."

They were right. The South did exist. It is not quite dead yet.

On his Southern tour, George Washington slept in a house on a street that already bore his name. A hundred forty years later, a little white girl, Myrtie Holliday, lived in that house on Washington Street. In the winter dark her mother would give her twenty-five cents, send her four blocks, through colored town, down to the oyster boat for a quart of shucked oysters. Nobody thought anything of it. She would be greeted by all, "Hey, Myrtie," and would greet in return. She knew them, and they knew her. The "spirit" (that is the way the colored folks put it; the white now might say "principle") of life was love. "In the North, a stranger is an enemy until proven otherwise; in the South he is a friend until proven otherwise." The people we are talking about were not strangers. That house is gone now, and so is the spirit of love. Law and order are gone, too. Colored folks say the spirit now is "hate."

Everybody knew everybody. It didn't matter how you dressed—everybody knew your character. The good people prevailed. They ran their neighborhoods. It was a Christian society. In the schools there was Chapel a few minutes every day, a Christmas program every year, perfect law and order and discipline, almost perfect politeness and manners. Our society was not controlled by law but by prescription; there was a prescribed code of conduct. We were not afraid of the law, we were afraid of the Lord. All levels of society subscribed to the code. We were not directed by law, but by manners.

White and colored worked together, lived close together in country and in town, saw each other every day, helped each other. The ones who needed help got help, local help. In our town there was no one large section where white lived and another where colored lived. There were small white and colored sections all mixed up. The richest folks in our town lived across the street from a colored section. One of the colored who lived across the street was also rich. Wiley Vines had started as a drayman hauling goods, then hauling kerosene oil. He bought some Standard Oil stock when they sold more kerosene than gasoline, and held it while gasoline sales caught fire. Relations within a single race could not have been more congenial than between the two. The white folks went to the white school, and the colored folks to the colored school. It did not seem to hurt anybody.

A Blue-Ribbon Committee of teachers (Harvard President James Bryant Conant was chairman, if I remember right) studied the schools in 1950, called them excellent, and suggested no changes. A year or two later, the Jacobin political court decided the politicians knew more, and forced the neither-eager races to mix. Since then, the schools have become worse each year than the one before: politics kills standards.

Medical care was cheap or free. The doctors, local boys and girls who came back to their home community, had a common interest and common feeling for their patients. Appointments were not made, the patient just went in, took a seat and got seen in turn except when a real sick one came in. We treated everybody who needed it, delivered all the babies in the county, at no cost to the taxpayer. We could handle most everything; when we needed a consultation we sent the patient to, or called, Duke. Duke was easy to get hold of—then; doctors were private, not government.

The most important element in medical care is to be able to talk to your doctor. Then, he knew your history before you started talking. You could talk to him and get more listening from him for nothing or for three dollars than you can get now for a thousand. The reason is simple, the patient was there because he wanted to get well, not because he wanted disability. There was a "shortage" of doctors, they could treat free; now there is a surplus. What is worse than a shortage of doctors? A surplus. The present system, an overfunded industry, has manufactured too many doctors, so they are looking for make-work and to milk the third-party. The present system has given us too many patients looking for a free ride. They take up a lot of time with their unnecessary lab tests and resistance to work. Who can blame them? One word from the doctor and he has a patient for life and they have a vacation for life.

The South may be dying, but a few memories survive. In 1999 Frank Barnes (colored) came into my office in Greenville, North Carolina. I did not know him. When I finished with him it was quitting time, about 6:00 o'clock. I asked him where he was from. "I have just moved here from Hartford, Connecticut. I retired after 25 years."

"How did you get down here?"

"I wanted to move back home. I was born near Ayden and stayed there until I was grown."

I asked him, "Did you know Dr. Grady Dixon?"

Happiness spread over his face. "Did I know Dr. Grady? I had ten brothers and sisters. He brought us into the world. For all our life, any problem we had we called Dr. Grady. He was a wonderful man. We loved him."

Willie Petway (colored) a patient from Fountain, was leaving my office. I asked him, "Did you know Dr. Beasley?" (Doctor Beasley dressed like a Philadelphia lawyer, lived across the street from his office, made his community happy for fifty years.) His face shone, "Yes, I knew Dr. Bruce, and I know that Dr. Bruce is the best man I have ever known." Catharine Taylor (colored), also from Fountain, when asked about Dr. Beasley, said "he took care of us all our life; there could not be no finer man."

The same character and dedication could be ascribed to Dr. Mewborn in Farmville, Dr. Basnight in Stokes, Joe Smith and K.B. Pace in Greenville, Henderson Irving in Eureka, Will Young in Wilson, McClellan in Maxton. To thousands more over the South. They worked for the patient, for love, not for a third-party payment. Doctor and patient had a common interest and feeling. Sad, those warm hearts are now reduced to a mildewed inscription on a cold stone.

About 1955, one Sunday after church and dinner of "The Gospel Bird" (fried chicken), my Daddy called me. A colored preacher had called him: At the end of the "Protracted Meeting" some of the boys had got to fighting. We met him and the boys at the office. They had not many abrasions; mostly cuts, it was a razor fight. We put them on the tables, one by one, and sewed, the preacher keeping us company as we worked. After two or three hours of enjoyable conversation, the sun lower, we finished, the floor was covered in sutures and bloody 4x4's. We sewed up ten or twelve of them. The preacher paid us something—less than seventy-five dollars, doctors could afford to treat cheap—and we parted. They were happy, we were happy, we were friends. Christian love.

Mrs. Maggie Woodard came from down the river—Woolard country. I asked her why she was named Woodard, an upriver name. She saw the humor, and enjoyed telling me that her husband came from up the river. An estimable colored woman, she was 89 the last time I saw her. She described reality. The medical school had come to our town, with its impressive might and mighty cost. She spoke the opinion of the community: "There are more doctors in the county now than there ever were, yet it is harder to see one than it ever was. When your dear old Daddy was here, and you wanted a doctor, all you had to do was send for him and he would come to your house." She paused, smiled, said, "And you could pay him when you felt like it."

The community was happy, nary a complaint about medical care. In the 1950s a Blue-Ribbon committee of eminents studied the condition of American medical care, pronounced it the best in the world. Shortly after, Lyndon Johnson inaugurated the government system that began the overfunding and overexpansion of the industry, the flood of immigrant doctors, surplus of doctors, the shortage of medical care, the reduced quality and access of medical care, and the raising of government patronage, corruption, debt, and discontent of doctor and patient. The difference in the two circumstances was obvious: first, a non-system of private, or free, care, then Dr. Lyndon Johnson's government system. The cost has skyrocketed, proving a crushing burden on society.

Experts had called education and medicine good. That they were bad had not occurred to them or to the churches. But it did occur to the politicians. They had the courts, and the army, the power to intervene. They made it bad. Ludwig von Mises demonstrated, and experience has proved, that all human transactions are better done by a free, non-system than by government. Medical care was better in quality, accessibility, and price when it was free. Free of government, and when necessary, free of charge. All human enterprises, all human action, under socialism are not merely inferior, they are counterproductive, and worse: destructive of society. Destructive of every element of life, including morals.

Is an ignoramus or a Jacobin going to tell me that medical care is better now? Except for the evolution of technology, which would have advanced faster and cheaper if unhampered by government.

My barber, Thad "Wood" Wooten, told me that when I was a wee child my Daddy carried me into his shop, said, "take care of my boy, Wood," left me there, departed to attend to some business, came back later and picked me up. Wood, or his partners, cut my hair through adolescence until I left town. When I came home I resumed my visits there, and stayed well into my old age. Wood lost an eye in a childhood accident. In his seventies I operated on him for cataract. I never slept very well the night before operating on a one-eyed person. His operation came out well and he saw good for twenty years until he died. The last time he cut my hair he was 92 years old, I had to go to his house. A colored man, he ran a barber shop for white folks. He told me he made more real money off twenty-five-cent haircuts than six-dollar ones. "The money was better then and so was the country," he said.

If black-white relations were bad in the old days, how come whites and blacks liked or loved one another in the old days, went to the same church, called each other "family?" How come today the old colored and white folks like each other? If things are better now, how come it is the young colored who hate the white? A white group is inciting them—using the socialist doctrine of hate. It is error, sad and destructive, that race has become attached to an unrelated sectional economic conflict.

The Jacobins attacked the South, all America, in the 19th century. To serve their desire for power Abraham Lincoln's party joined with the Radicals (Civil Rights, Feminism, Statism, all the "isms" in the Radical club now called "Liberal") and stirred discord. They divided, they conquered. They replaced the Christian Gospel of Love with the Jacobin doctrine of hate. For power, they divided the regions, tried to divide the races, eagerly started America's bloodiest war, waged it in a selfish and vicious manner, and killed a republic in favor of an empire. They tried to make black hate white but the "vaccination" did not take.

Because of the War both races suffered terribly, together. Once the army left, they gradually recovered and made the South a happy place to live. They remained a close social unit for another hundred years. Yankee writers, including the premier Henry James, came south after the War and concluded that the South was indeed different from the materialist North, was a better place, of noble philosophy, of higher values.

The government has replaced God. In the first half of the last century the government monster was only an imp, its evil still small but growing. Satan is full-grown now.

In my youth I never heard a disparaging word about Abraham Lincoln. I am sorry to say our schools had the same books, the same lessons, as the Yankees. What I studied was the orthodox Lincoln: a poor, shy boy, painfully honest, who from childhood shone like a beacon in the darkness of his obscurity; he read by firelight, educated himself, aspired to nothing but Christian service; he lived a life of noble humility, saved his country when the duty was thrust upon him; died a martyr to the cause of human betterment. The ultimate Christian. After high school I went on to an education in science: mathematics, physics, chemistry, and biology. In medical school it was first the study of man's structure—his form, gross and microscopic. Then his function, how that structure worked. Then came diseases, how something in that structure went wrong.

Not a mention was made of Abraham Lincoln. It was a world he did not enter. Study filled all available time, a steady search for truth.

The doctor, like the farmer, works in reality, looks for truth.

Then I embarked on the clinical practice of medicine. A busy time. We worked. I saw doctors and nurses who served, to the best of their ability, really served the needs of the sick. They had a common feeling and a common interest with their patients, really cared for them, motivated by duty unsullied by an intervening third party. It was a non-system—a transaction between two people. I saw people who earned their living by hard work producing valuable products, lived in the real world, and had sturdy character. I came to know those patients, the unknown private citizens, who carry this country. It was a Christian-based society. They were good, and that was why America was strong. I, too, esteemed those doctors, nurses, farmers, artisans, store keepers. The government was not involved in life in those days. Medical care and commerce, all human interactions, were private. People were producers, not consumers. It was a world of working folks, not of Lincolns. I never thought of Abraham Lincoln.

A doctor doesn't have much time, but he can pick up a book between patients at night. I began to read non-medical writings. One subject was American History. Roanoke Island and Jamestown led to the struggle of the Colonies striving for independence from Britain, and that to the Southern *de facto* colonies striving for independence from the North. That is America's fundamental story and description of America's character. The two leading figures, George Washington and Abraham Lincoln, were on opposite sides. America's premier figure— "Honest Abe"—whatever he was, was no doctor, no nurse, and no farmer. He planted no crops, sowed only division, bound up no wounds. In his two careers—lawyer, politician—he was not looking for reality or truth, he was hunting empire. No producer, he was a destroyer.

There were two Lincolns—the myth and the man. The man is dead; the myth lives. The war he made was no myth. The War to Prevent Southern Independence is a cancer in the very living marrow of America.

The Aim of This Work

"Who controls the present controls the past, who controls the past controls the future."

—GEORGE ORWELL

Do justice to the dead.
If you cannot muster piety,
Give them justice.
It is their due.

THE AIM OF THIS STUDY is to discover Historical Truth. Oh Truth, you jewel, you priceless treasure, after four hundred years of American history, now lost. America's power elite have buried the old truths, are busy covering over the present ones, and writing fables for the future. Truth, cowering in the catacombs, has less influence now than at any time since the nation came ashore at Jamestown. A nation is a people with a common history. That history is being deliberately murdered, that identity buried, and a new, false image put in its place. Beyond the end of a vicious century Americans suffer not mere "Politically Correct" thought, but sheer "Thought Control."

An elite faction, by the collusion of private wealth and government might, are able to distort what America was, and invent what it is, in order to possess what it will be.

This book corrects that error. The War to Prevent Southern Independence defines America. The nation cannot be known without it. The national character is given in the answer to a question: "War—Why?"

Ten thousand years after the Ice Age a second cataclysm struck America, more devastating than the first, and not an Act of God. Natural disasters—events beyond human control—are not the major cause of human pain, but terrors willfully brought. The chief enemy of man is man. There are men who, to raise themselves, to subordinate their fellows, will kill their fellows.

America's supreme cataclysm was its supreme calamity. A war. War—the worst of human horrors. The palliating poet said, "And the war came." The war did not come, it was brung, the poetic Lincoln went to considerable effort to bring it. Not "came," but brought, inflicted, with deliberate design and calculated conspiracy.

Seven score years ago our stepfather brought forth on this continent a war, a war more devastating than all its other misfortunes—natural and man-made—combined. He destroyed two-thirds of Southern wealth. He killed a million of his own people—more than all their other wars added together. A fourth to a third of Southern soldiers were counted dead, not considering the vast uncounted in that informal army, or the thousands who died later. Civilian deaths were pandemic, impossible to reckon. Perhaps a fourth of the colored people, slave and free, died during or as result of the war. Southern census showed the only population decrease in America's history. In the South a whole generation was blighted, their posterity afflicted for years.

In the North one soldier in ten died, not much troubling Northern society, so many being poor mercenaries—domestic and imported, 250,000 foreign born, so many the Pope protested. Foreign and domestic, black and white, joined not for principle but for bounty, some by force. A fourth of the entire Federal war expenditure went for buying their enlistment, unprecedented in any other American war.

As cataclysm the war stands supreme. No other event, no combination of events, equals that war in measure of change it effected. Gigantic in size, it was all bad. It extinguished property, economy, wealth, social order, health, and life in magnitude unapproached by other national calamities. Just a part of the war, Sherman's march, is ranked fourth among severest ecological disasters.

Physical damage was confined to the South. Moral damage was far worse in the North. "To the victors belong the spoils"—and also the moral spoliation conferred by "power, plunder, and extended rule." So deep was the rot that the Northern glittering period that came out of it was labeled forever "The Gilded Age." Adversity being the only builder of character, defeat spared the Southern people the moral decay.

The moral injury was not limited to individuals, it weakened institutions, and worse to say—it killed the body politic. The magnificent social and political body born in 1607, little altered by name change in 1776, was destroyed in the holocaust, consumed, and burnt down. That injury was far-reaching and permanent.

From the ashes of death a new life always arises, and so it did in America. The old country, governed by a limited power, was gone.

Rising in its place was not a phoenix of hope, but a bird of prey. Abraham Lincoln brought forth a different species, no new nation, but a new government. The victors destroyed their own country.

Truth cries to be found. Don't look to the government to find it. It is they who have kidnapped and hid it. Government is the captor of truth, its officers stifling truth to tighten their hold on power.

To promote their selfish interest the United States Government had mandated Thought Control.

Government of the people by the people is government by consent of the governed, self-determined, not ruler-determined; it is government local in place, limited in power. Abraham Lincoln forced on his people a consolidated government, of power rudely seized in the talons of the central authority.

If Communist means total government ownership—complete socialism, then America is not Communist. If Fascist means subtotal government ownership—incomplete socialism, a fusion of big government and big money—then America is surely Fascist. The United States are now governed by a union of government and their elite friends ostensibly outside, who own money—private power.

Directly or indirectly, through private and government power, the same people who control our government control every opinion shaping institution—government agencies, public agenda, movies, television, newspapers, magazines, book publishing, education curricula, schools, colleges. "Veritas" still adorns university seals but is banished from academe. Wisdom has no tenure. The universities have made football professional and freedom proscribed. The faculty are servile. They teach government doctrine.

Government has created its own self-serving fiction. It writes its own history. It defines itself. It determines its own power. Name one single power the United States Government does not now possess. Name one large newspaper not in a league with the Democratic Party. The other party? They do not even have a newspaper; they are paper, an image of power. We are on the edge of one-party government.

We shall have to find the truth ourselves. This book gives it. But who will read it? It has no sponsor, plenty of opponents. The Jacobins will condemn it, slaves disdain it, and the mass ignore it. What a shame, this story is reality. Truth is better than lies. It is necessary if people want to be free.

A cataclysm has its majesty, an epoch its wonder. A rising and a falling both have their moments of brilliance. Even death can have nobility as well as obscenity. That war displays the infinite extremes of human character, from the Hellish inferno of the ruler's selfish pride to the sublime heights of self-sacrificing principle—the lowest and the highest a person, and a people, can ascend and descend.

All Americans suffer from that war, but not many know why. Only a very few understand it. It is the very essence of the national character. The heroic character of George Washington notwithstanding, America's second independence war far exceeds the importance of the first. The Southern War is the national Iliad. It is the American classic. Every scholar must know it or renounce claim to scholarship. Every citizen is duty-bound to study it, in piety to a deserving ancestry and obligation to a needful posterity.

Beyond American piety is the need of all people to learn it. Its lessons are not just for Americans, they are for all men everywhere.

It shows each individual what men with power can do to him.

Everybody knows history repeats itself. It repeats itself because nobody reads its lesson. Read this lesson: a chapter at a time. To make the burden easy each chapter will stand alone. Skip around; read a few minutes whatever chapter calls your interest. Maybe none of it does. Then make yourself read it. Read it fifteen times and you will begin to understand its importance. Learning is repetition is repetition. Read it, learn it, try to recruit people willing to know and able to care, so that you can make a change. It takes knowledge, virtue, and courage. Knowledge to know, virtue to care, courage to stand. Not an easy task. Knowledge is not common. Which is rarer —virtue or courage? To find the three combined together is almost a miracle.

This story is of use. Its lessons learned will prevent future pain. It is the only defense against people whose private ambitions will destroy freedom, prosperity, and life. Sinful man must be restrained in power over his fellows.

"Why must we study the past? Because it is all we have."
—JOHN LUKACS

"Everyone should do all in his power to collect and disseminate the truth, in the hope that truth may find a place in history and descend to posterity. History is not relation of campaigns and battles and generals, but that which shows principles."
—ROBERT E. LEE——

A War to Prevent Southern Independence: Why?

"Quis custodiet Custodes?" ("Who will be custodian of the Custodians? Who will watch the watchmen, govern the governors?")

—JUVENAL, "SATIRES" VI, 347

"In all free states the Evil to be avoided is Tyranny, that is to say, the summa imperial, unlimited power, solely in the hands of the One, or the Few, or the Many."

—JONATHAN SWIFT, "CONTESTS AND DISSENSIONS IN ATHENS AND ROME"

"The Gettysburg Address is poetry not sense. Its doctrine is that Lincoln's soldiers sacrificed their lives for the cause of self-determination: 'that government of the people, by the people, for the people' should not perish from the earth. It is difficult to imagine anything more untrue. Lincoln's soldiers actually fought against self-determination. It was the Confederates who fought for the right of the people to govern themselves."

—H.L. MENCKEN

WHY WAR? THAT IS THE QUESTION. Of all the questions about America's epic and epoch, the war that ended government by the people in the United States– the essential question is: Why? Why was it fought?

That question needs to be answered. Not just for America, the answers apply to all mankind, everywhere, and forever. They are universal, eternal. They discover the permanent things.

What was the cause of the war? Why did they fight, North and South?

The question can be focused: "Southern Independence—Why War?" Why did some states choosing independence cause somebody else to choose war? The answer to that question describes America's character and fundamental event. It gives perfect instruction in man's attempt to order his group life by what is called government—to create a civilized society. It describes the successes and the eventual failure of that effort, and tells clearly what kind of government is necessary to protect man from man.

The Southern independence story reveals the very nature of man, of mankind, the essence of life itself. It is more than classical; it is Biblical in dimension. Its lessons answer life's fundamental questions. Its lessons are necessary if freedom is to survive.

The Confederate States of America is the story of the first principle of government—the necessity to limit power.

The cause of the war was not regional differences. The two sections were different and had been different since the second colony (Massachusetts Puritans) was established. But regional differences are not war. Differences are one thing, killing quite another. Differences did not necessitate war before time, nor in 1861. Why then, war?

The Southerners merely defended themselves. The last thing the South wanted was war with so large a foe. All the South wanted was independence. "Let us go in peace" was Jefferson Davis's plea to the Senate. The South had no choice. Threatened, attacked, and invaded, they had to fight.

The North fought because their president—one single man—started a war. Lincoln had promised a high tariff. On March 2, 1861, the United States signed into law the Morrill tariff, the highest ever—60% on some articles. On March 11, the

Confederate States of America enacted a 5% tariff. The next day the money party—Northern merchants, manufacturers, bankers—demanded war. Bad enough that an independent South would deprive them of the protective tariff and tax-free existence, but far worse, the tariff differential would move Northern trade to low-duty Southern ports. Southern independence could not be allowed. The only way to prevent losing Southern money was by war. Only the money men demanded war. The Abolitionists at first opposed it.

Without war, Lincoln's party would die. When seeking office Lincoln agitated conflict, when elected he blocked settlement, when inaugurated he planned and executed a conspiracy to make a war. Then he used self-conferred war powers to drag the Northern people into it.

Why did he do it? Lord Russell, British Foreign Secretary, answered in a public speech in October 1861: "The Party of Lincoln is fighting for empire, sir—power and territory." The Providence, Rhode Island, *Daily Post*, on 13 April, 1861, said: "We are to have war because Abraham Lincoln loves a Party better than he loves his country." The war was America's grand epoch, changing forever the life of every person living then or born later. No American living today—400-year native or just off the boat or plane, escapes the results of that war. He lives in a country far different from what it was designed to be, and would be but for that war. The war shattered the citizen's defenses against the despotism of government power. Because of the cataclysm that was the War to Prevent Southern Independence, he lives now a mere subject of a socialist, omni-competent state.

Mankind are not solitary, they choose to live in groups. A group must have government. Government, to conduct its business, must have officers. Ah, there's the rub: officers like office more than they like people. "Public servant" means "Officer served by the public." Given power, they take more. Unless chained, officers will chain those who served them power to do it. This story tells what government really is, how government really operates. This story is called History. History gives its lessons clear. Few have learned it.

Tyranny is illegal seizure of power; despotism is illegal exercise of power. Government has the means to take power: the purse and the stick—the money to buy friends and the force to punish enemies. It will use those powers to take more. Power can be controlled only by an opposing power. Every government must be constructed so that power is limited by a counter power or it will always end in tyranny.

The first principle of government is: it must be limited. Wise men say so:

All government actions are counterproductive (James Buchanan, Nobel Laureate).

All government actions are destructive (Ludwig von Mises).

Government acts only through force, thus must be despotic (Frederic Bastiat).

Government is the conduct of public affairs for private gain (Axel Oxenstierne).

The Confederates understood that the essential element of government is the limitation of it, not the form. The form will not save you. Democracy is no protection. It is always commanded by an inner elite. It is they who benefit and control it. All political parties are corrupt. The multitudes who vote for a party are not the party. In their devotion to party they surrender their freedom.

Government officers will violate the law in proportion to their power. Little power—little harm; large power—unlimited harm, as in the violence of 1861-1877 and the 20th century. Freedom can exist only when central government is limited, when power is kept in possession of private citizen and local government. Freedom is only one thing: the due administration of the law. Big government will always break the law. Because it can. Every group must construct their government according to the known laws of group life. Or pay the price. When the chains on government are loosened the governors tighten the chains on the people. Chain the governors, not the people. Government must be controlled, restrained by retaining most power at home.

George Washington begged the citizens of the recently united States to govern themselves by electing individual virtuous men to office, to refrain from the making of parties. Washington did not want faction government—made by a party and ruled by an elite. He entreated the people to not form interest groups seeking special privilege at the expense of others, preferment for one class. He warned that patronage at the expense of their fellow citizens would destroy the republic. His plea and his warning were ignored. Factions formed immediately. The Northern mercantile party used their majority control of Congress to enact measures that subsidized Northern commerce men at Southern farmer expense. The tariff, national bank, and so-called "internal improvements" that so injured the South were examples of party greed and factional aggression.

Washington's two pleas: Avoid faction (party), and foreign entanglements. History—experience—has shown that those twin evils have been the ruin of republican government.

Most professional politicians are politicians because they care for power, not for principle or people. Public service means the public serves them. The average citizen does not realize how large are the rewards of office, or how far some men will go to win them. Ambition—the desire to subordinate others—is the Devil's Proposition: Worldly Power.

Much of Lincoln's party "were in it for power, plunder, and extended rule." So said Ward Hill Lamon, the man Lincoln most trusted in Washington City. Lamon was Lincoln's aide, not one of his party radicals like Charles Sumner, clubbed with Lincoln for rule.

The Gettysburg Address: A pretty little song made of the words of other men. A string of American slogans set to rhythm. Like its author, "strong on style, weak in substance." A tale told by an actor, signifying nothing. Seven score years ago Father Abraham brought forth a new rule, conceived in self and dedicated to the proposition that all men are equal subjects.

Douglas Southall Freeman, son of a member of the Rockbridge Artillery, editor of the *Richmond News Leader*, author of the most esteemed biographies of Washington and Lee, was a sincere, modest Southern gentleman. Every morning on his way to work, alone in the three o'clock darkness of Richmond's Monument Avenue, he saluted the statue of Robert E. Lee, the Christian model. Every year, on her birthday, he saluted in his paper Lucy Chandler, who cradled the wounded Stonewall Jackson brought to her house for refuge, a model of the self-sacrificing Southern women. He saluted the South as a Christian, that is, moral-based society, and the Confederacy as an obligatory defense of self-government.

Another Southern lady, exceeded by none in character, was Mrs. Annie Wilson James Covington, inheritor of Jackson's bloody handkerchief, cousin of Jubal Early and Jeb Stuart, and a friend of Dr. Freeman. He took her and me over the Seven Days Battle. We saw the tardiness of Jackson, the failure of Huger and Magruder. It was an exhilarating day.

America's most momentous event, a cataclysm that murdered a republic and birthed an empire, has never been allowed its correct name. The man who made the bloodiest of America's wars first called it no war at all, merely an "insurrection." He had to call it not a war because the war-making power belongs to Congress alone. In 1848 Abraham Lincoln declared that the president has no right to make a war and that any people had a right to independence. The Constitution grants the Federal Government right to enter a state only at the request of the governor or legislature. But an independent South would cost his party its existence and control of Southern finance. Force—war—was the only way the party could keep its life and its backers their larceny.

Their war became so big they could no longer call it a riot, so they called it a "civil" war to label their resisters as traitors.

It could not be a "civil" war because:

1. A civil war is two groups fighting for possession of a government. One group wants to take the other's place. The

South had no desire to destroy, overthrow, or possess the Federal Government; they just wanted to escape it.

2. Sovereign states cannot engage in a "civil" war. The states were pronounced "sovereign" by the British Government, by foreign nations, and by their own documents. No State surrendered its sovereignty or was thought to have done so. Nobody suggested that membership was compulsory.

3. By joint resolution of both houses, on March 28, 1928, Congress established that the official name of the war of 1861-1865 shall be "The War Between the States." Not an evil name but still wrong.

The war was fought for one reason: to prevent Southern Independence. Its only correct name is "The War to Prevent Southern Independence."

Abraham Lincoln did more damage to America than any other man, native or foreign. He found it a republic and left it an empire. He forced on his people the most vicious enemy of the people—consolidated government. Consolidated power always kills freedom, makes wars, and kills people. Lincoln broke the laws. No pretense of words—"equality," "patriotism," even "freedom"—saves freedom. Freedom can live only under limited government. Lincoln's deeds put the socialist doctrine of hate in place of the Christian gospel of love. He made war, the worst of human terrors, the very worst expression of hate.

Lincoln's army did not fight for government by the people; they fought for government by the ruler. Government by the people is government by consent of the governed. In the federal system it is called State rights: protector of minorities. The comic Mort Sahl once remarked that the only thing saving the U.S. from Fascism was the Southern mistrust of big government.

The War to Prevent Southern Independence is a detective story, containing an autopsy on a murder victim—the government, and an examination of an injured victim—the nation. One dead, the other, mortally wounded.

The Confederate flag was first raised by an abused minority. "Let us go in peace," was their plea. They were not allowed to go in peace. They were invaded by their abusers to prevent escape. Attacked, for no reason but selfish rule—party power and money—they were forced to defend themselves. The flag's principle, government by the people, was affirmed when six more states, not themselves attacked, followed the flag to refuse the tyrant's war of usurpation. All the states should have joined. There were protests of his criminal war in all the states.

The Confederate flag means only one thing: the never-finished fight to limit government. The Confederate flag has nothing to do with slavery, it means freedom from slavery. Salute the Confederate flag, it stands for freedom. The Confederate flag stands for the never-ending struggle of the people to defend themselves from their rulers. Revere the flag. Its Christian cross is the perfect symbol of resistance to the Devil's Proposition—worldly power. The humble Saint Andrew's Cross. The banner was stainless. It still is.

The Confederate flag, like its nation, conceived by necessity, was made in urgent haste, stitched together under fire. Artists call it beautiful, in form and principle. Raised first by one nation, it now is seen in many, emblem of the eternal struggle of the small against the large, of right resisting might, of citizens betrayed by their own officers, of victim versus parasite. A banner international of freedom.

That is the meaning of the Confederate flag.

"Appomattox was a greater defeat for liberty than Waterloo was a victory."

—LORD ACTON

"The consolidation of the states into one vast union, sure to be increasingly despotic at home and dangerously adventurous abroad, will lead to certain ruin."

—ROBERT E. LEE, 1866

"There is another reason to persevere. If we are defeated, to our punishments will be added the injury of truth. We shall be forced to drain the last bitter dregs from our cup of humiliation and read the story of our struggle written by New England historians."

—JEFFERSON DAVIS, JANUARY 1865

"Our own rulers do us more harm than any foreign ones."

—DANIEL HACKNEY

Killing the Union

"To kill one's fellow creatures needs no good genius. To calm, not make, a tempest, to exercise prudence and judgment, that is the worthy achievement."

—ERASMUS, LETTER TO BISHOP TRENT, 1530

"Abraham Lincoln has no right to a soldier in Fort Sumter. A series of states think they should have a separate government. They have a right to decide that question without appealing to you and me. Standing with the principles of '76 behind us, who can deny that right?"

—ABOLITIONIST WENDELL PHILLIPS, NEW BEDFORD, MASS., APRIL 9, 1861

"The South wants independence, the North wants empire."

—LONDON TIMES, NOVEMBER 7, 1861

"What they really want is civil war... The President of the United States holds the destiny of the country in his hands ... War will be averted unless he is overruled by the disunion faction of his party. We all know the irrepressible conflict that is going on in his camp. Will they use patriotism to manufacture partisan capital, to take party advantage? Throw aside this party squabble about how you are going to get along with your party. Peace is the only policy that can save this country."

—STEPHEN A. DOUGLAS, U.S. SENATE, MARCH 1861

OVER AND OVER AGAIN ABRAHAM Lincoln declared that he went to war for one reason and one reason only: to preserve the Union. The claim is impossible, absurd. Impossible because nothing is preserved by destroying it. Absurd and a lie because he pursued office by agitating disunion; when elected he blocked all negotiation; as soon as he was sworn in he went immediately to work to design a stratagem and direct a conspiracy to make war.

Lincoln's invasion of Charleston Harbor, calling up an army, levying troops, declaring war upon the seceded states—caused six more states to secede. How did that "save the Union"? If he had not made war, those states would have remained in the union. They refused to join his unconstitutional war. Lincoln sent in troops, established military control of state governments, arrested state officials, scattering them in unknown prisons. He ordered the arrest of Maryland legislators; the Chief Justice of the United States protested and Lincoln ordered his arrest. Kentucky and Missouri did secede, but could not prevail because of Lincoln's army occupation.

How did his war save the Union? How can Lincoln claim to be defending the Union when the South was merely pulling away? The South was running away, the North was invading. Whom was he defending? What was he defending? Secession was a right specified or inferred by all ratifiers of the Constitution, denied by none, claimed by New England, taught at West Point.

"Union" was simply the businessmen's war cry. When South Carolina seceded only the money men cried, "The Union cannot be broken." "The Union must be preserved" meant "The Tariff must be preserved." Their only excuse for war was "Union." No one, not even they, connected slavery to war. The Abolitionists themselves at first asked for peace, censured the businessmen for their greedy motive.

Edmund Wilson in *Patriotic Gore* said that the greatest good fortune of Lincoln's life was his luck that the Northern people accepted his notion of "Union," a concept of value only to him and his party. The people accepted his construction of events, that their choice lay only between joining him in his war or suffering something worse. They accepted his new "Union," a form of government, radically different from the one originally founded. "Radical" comes from a Latin word "radix," meaning "root." Radical means tear out by the roots. His new "Union" was not the old Union; it was radical usurpation.

William Herndon, his office mate and law partner of twenty-four years, knew him best. Herndon said that Lincoln used a friend like an orange: when he had taken all the use out of that friend he would throw away the friend like an orange peel. Lincoln used "Union" for what good it did him and threw the rest of it away. Power seekers use words to gain their ends. Fellow lawyers and politicians said that all Lincoln's words, public and private, were studied, never candid, always to a purpose, spoken with affected sincerity. Artfully, he masked substance with style. Lincoln's "Union" was only "cant." (Latin: a "chant" or a "song," mere words without meaning; affected, hypocritical use of a pious term for a purpose.) He used "Union" as a sentimental memory, an image called up of a thing once good. It was a term serving only himself. He had extinguished the old union, destroying the real definition of "Union." His "Union" was no longer a federal union of sovereign states.

The poet Edgar Lee Masters, who was from Lincoln's home territory in Illinois, wrote of the Gettysburg Address: "Is it possible that Lincoln believed what he said? His musical, meaningless words are just opposite to the truth. The soldiers honored in the cemetery had not died for government by the people. Lincoln's army was fighting for consolidated government ... It was the unburied, their bones scattered and scorned around Gettysburg—the Confederate soldiers—who died for government by the people."

The Declaration of Independence, the British Government, and the Articles of Confederation defined the people of each state as sovereign. They formed a federal republic whose aim was liberty—freedom from outside rule. It was a compact of separate states who joined voluntarily, with never a thought that their right to leave it would be questioned. New York, Massachusetts,

Virginia, others declared, and all implied, that they retained their sovereignty, that they could withdraw at will.

If one had the right they all had it. In ratifying the Constitution, no state surrendered its independent sovereignty. Had it been suggested, no state would have signed; they had just obtained their independence from England; they certainly did not intend to take on a heavier yoke. All of them affirmed their sovereignty by their ratification resolutions. Massachusetts demonstrated its belief in secession by threatening to withdraw on several occasions. There is no freedom in any association without right to withdraw.

Alexis de Tocqueville said, "The Union was formed by the voluntary agreement of the states. And these, in uniting together, have not forfeited their sovereignty, nor have they been reduced to the condition of one and the same people. If one of the states chose to withdraw its name from the contract, it would be difficult to disprove its right of doing so, and the Federal Government would have no means of maintaining its claims directly, either by force or by right."

If one cannot withdraw from an organization then one has no freedom. When one party violates a contract, the other must have a right to withdraw from it.

Lincoln made his monstrous war to benefit nobody but his party. He could find no excuse but the false excuse of "Union." "Union," a nonexistent thing, he made divine. He gave to a name, to a mere word, a life, a character of its own. He made a word holy. "A rose by any name would smell as sweet," Shakespeare wrote, because whatever you call it a rose is still a rose. But what is "Union?" What does it do? To whom is it accountable? Is it a god? Murray Rothbard said Lincoln sent his army into the South, pillaging and murdering on behalf of a pagan idol, "Union," a "Moloch demanding human sacrifice to sustain its power and its glory." Lincoln's "Union" was not that agreement among the states to operate under the Constitution he had sworn to obey. His "Union" was not united to the lives and happiness of the people he had sworn to protect.

What is a union sewed together by bayonets? What is a union that devastates half a country, destroys three-fourths of the area's wealth, kills a million people? What is a "Union" that obliterates the once-happy association of sovereign parts, that demolishes forever the federal concept of diffused power and limited government, without which there can be no freedom? He killed freedom—the reason for, the essence of, and the guarantee of, the real union.

Is a word—"Union"—somehow superior to property, to liberty, to a human life?

Abraham Lincoln's "Union" was a new thing, a different system of government. In the old nation power belonged to the people as private citizens or in their local governments. Lincoln's new government usurped power, seized it, consolidated it into a single central authority. And he was the authority. "Union" now meant "Tyranny." The practical definition of Lincoln's "Union" was Abraham Lincoln and the Republican Party. A party is not the voters, it is the elite at its top. His politicians were empowered, his Northern money men were enriched. They were its beneficiaries. All other people were its victims. What good did Lincoln's new union do any of the men who died in his army? What good did it do the men who served in his army? What good did it do their families? What good did Lincoln's new union do any citizen living then—or now? "Union" was a cynical slogan for conquest.

Lincoln did not have to go to war. There was no demand, not even desire, for war by the Northern people, rather a universal hope for peace. Even most Northern businessmen did not want war. Lincoln's party felt differently. After Lincoln's election the money men began to see that an independent South would cost them their monopolies, tariff subsidy, captive market, and exemption from taxes. The flow of money from the South to the North would reverse direction. The money men and Republican politicians went immediately to Lincoln and demanded war.

Southerners understood the situation. Thomas Clingman of North Carolina told the Senate weeks before Fort Sumter, on March 19, 1861: "Lincoln will not call Congress into session because if he would ask them to go to war against the Confederate

States. I do not believe they would agree to do it. The Republicans intend ... as soon as they can collect a force, to have a war, to begin, and then call Congress suddenly together and say 'The honour of the country is concerned; the flag is insulted. You must come up and vote men and money.'"

The Northern Democrats understood this also, as the above quotation from Stephen A. Douglas indicates.

That is when Lincoln's statesmanship was tested. If the practical meaning of union had mattered to Lincoln, if union had really meant anything to that politician, he would have reined in his vanity, bridled his ambition, loved his people more than his power, done his duty, and kept the peace. But, peace would have killed his party. So he gave his party a life-saving war. He gave his country a life-killing war. The Southern people were never a threat to the peace and security of the North. But the North let stand Lincoln's senseless, selfish excuse of "Union." "The 'Union' is in danger. Join me in my war!" They heard the call, but they did not see the poison under the eagle's wings—"I am the Union." ("*L'Etat, c'est moi.*)" Lincoln had changed forever the nature of the American union. Before their very eyes the American people were presented with a revolution. But, they had not eyes to see. They accepted his new "Union," now meaningless in definition, vicious in action, destructive in result.

He was no unionist anyway. All his life his practice was to incite disunion, to seek notice by stirring strife and discord, not unity and amity. He was an agitator, what the Communists call an "activist." Political eminence comes from roiling the waters, not by calming them.

The most partisan, strident, and divisive member of the Illinois Legislature, the only unity Lincoln ever sought therein or thereafter was party unity; he would shed even that when it threatened his career. He saw every subject in party terms, working always to divide the rival party. His method was to reduce all subjects to slogans, metaphors, quotations. The method was effective because it was familiar and simple. It was effective, but untrue. His party strategy was "Be ever so careful not to notify the enemy."

"A house divided cannot stand." That trite appeal to his party for unity had dignity conferred upon it when he used that Bible text speech to frighten and divide the nation. It was his method: familiar words misused, high-sounding, taken by the public to be profound because biblical. In the first place it was untrue—the nation had stood divided for two hundred fifty years. Such a condition is called liberty. In the second place he changed and distorted Jesus's meaning. That vague statement was taken for gospel because it came from the Gospel, but it was meaningless, false, foolish, self-serving, and dangerous. It was absurd—who divided the house more than he did? It was only a slogan. It helped him but it bled the nation.

As much as he urged unity on his party, Lincoln pushed division in his politics. Outside the party he was quick to cry, "I view with alarm," whenever he could indict a rival. Even within the party he was divisive in competing with other candidates for place. He urged a one-term limit on his party's congressmen while he was seeking the seat, never mentioning it again when he at last gained it. So much a disunionist was he in his one term in Congress, pursuing notice to gain place, that he embarrassed his own party, which refused to renominate him. When the false issue of Kansas-Nebraska presented itself in 1854 he leaped at the opportunity to agitate disunion in order to win public notice and to advance himself at the expense of public order. His Bloomington speech in 1856, Springfield speech in 1858, and his Cooper Union speech in 1860 were provocatively disunionist, promoting discord to promote himself. All those rabble rousings were done in an election year, mere rhetoric to win an election.

Lincoln's "Union" was no more than what John Randolph called "the unprincipled conduct of ambitious men." Self-interest pretending to be principle.

His campaign for president was based entirely upon disunion, looking for every opportunity to gain attention, to arouse sectional animosity, to frighten the Northerners, to polarize the voters for benefit of his party. Elected, he goaded the South and blocked all conciliation and negotiation. Inaugurated, he went right to work to relieve "the most anxious time of my life" by starting the war.

"Union" was a slogan to raise his party that brought down his country.

Love of money was the root of the evil that first injured the nation with the false issue of "slavery." To hold power his party would kill two nations with another false issue—"Union." There was no valid reason for war. The only excuse Lincoln could find was "Union." The worst of human terrors—war—waged for a word. A word the meaning of which he killed. Making the war was dishonest. Making war against Americans was treason.

Abraham Lincoln did not save the union. He killed the union. He murdered the federal republic and set in its place the empire. To esteem Abraham Lincoln is to respect words, not deeds. Those who live by the pen envy their colleague who rose to the greater glory of the sword.

"This is our second war for independence. All we want is independence. Our assailants want war. When New England was in distress we sent them relief and supplies. They repay us now with invasion and bullets."

—THOMAS J. JACKSON

"Where is the war to come from? From any Southern state? When the North talks war do they mean the South will make war on the North? Certainly not. All we want is peace.

—SENATOR ALBERT G. BROWN OF MISSISSIPPI, MARCH 1861

"The man who shall inaugurate war will be the greatest murderer that ever disgraced the form of man, will go down to his grave covered with the curses of Heaven and the cries of thousands of widows and orphans."

—SENATOR JOEL LANE OF OREGON, MARCH 1861

"On the day the American people accepted Abraham Lincoln's invasion of a sovereign state the Republic died and the Empire was born."

—WASHINGTON POST, 1905

Sectional Differences

"Cultivators of the earth are the most valuable citizens. They are the most vigorous, the most independent, the most virtuous. They are tied to their country and wedded to its liberty and interests by the most lasting bonds. I consider manufacturers as panders of vice, and generally the instruments by which the liberties of a country are overturned."

—THOMAS JEFFERSON, WRITING FROM PARIS, AUGUST 23, 1785

"The interests of the North and the South are different, not merely different, they are antagonistic."

—GEORGE MASON

"The [Northern politicians] joined Jefferson's Party for expedient reasons. They cared no more for Southern principles of small, honest government than the money party."

—HENRY ADAMS (PARAPHRASE)

SENATOR WILLIE P. MANGUM of North Carolina, after a visit to Boston, wrote to a constituent on October 7, 1834: "The principles of our Federative system have not taken root among the Northern party. They hardly comprehend them. The basis of that party is naked interest. Principles are trifles compared to pecuniary interest. If the policy of New England prevails it will destroy our system of government.

"We have nothing to hope from New England. I fear their settled, steady, and persevering policy. Their Federal policy is selfish, sure to destroy the Federal system.

"Their majority in Congress increases. Power in this Country is concentrated in the fangs of an interested majority, remorseless, heartless. The brutal tariff of 1828–32 found us powerless to combat it. What have we to hope when they next raise it? When the North enacts a high tariff, enforced by armed might, the union will have been killed.

"Our Northern brethren know how to say pleasant words to the traveler from the South, much better than we do, to soothe and secure our support for measures alien to the interest of the South. Boston is civil to strangers, yet all the time you feel the ice. There is little of that frank, happy, and cordial impulse that enables one to look into the heart of our Southern people.

"The South has before her a high and glorious destiny, if allowed to achieve it. We are the real conservators of our political system. Only true Federalism, State Rights, will preserve liberty. Standing in the way of liberty are power, office, patronage, bribery. Venality, stupidity, personal ambition must not supersede principle. Liberty can be preserved only if we have sufficient character to put her defense before all else."

Historians like to say that the war was caused by sectional differences. There were wide differences in space between the two sections and wide distances in character. The people were different and did not know each other. A soldier in the Federal army wrote from Virginia to his parents back in New York: "The Southern people look just like we do!" He had heard so much anti-South propaganda he expected to see monsters.

Their differences were long standing, from their origin in England. New England was founded by people from East Anglia, that part of England northeast of London. As in New England later, they had a denser population, larger towns, a more mercantile society conducive to the commerce and manufacturing which they learned from the highly-developed Dutch just across the North Sea. Calvinism, a stern, punishing religion, took hold there. They made and followed Cromwell in politics. The early Southern settlers came mostly from the area around London, the Channel Coast, and the Midlands. They were farmers, not merchants, Anglicans, not Puritans, of a more tolerant religion, not so harsh toward their neighbors, more accepting of pleasure and enjoyment of life. They were Cavaliers loyal to Charles, not Puritans following Cromwell. The two sides had already fought each other before they came to America. That war had been forgotten, that difference had subsided. It did not make them start a war in America.

Maybe not entirely, for the Puritans brought with them Cromwell's delight in punishing the "other." Southerners never sought to interfere with, control, exploit, or punish Northerners, but the reverse was not true.

Different in the Old World, their economies grew further apart with the passage of time in the New. In New England and the North circumstances gradually made their economy into an urban, commercial, manufacturing economy. Farmers became city folks. Factories multiplied and a bit later immigrants to work them were brought over in great numbers from Europe.

Their merchants built great fortunes from three monopolies:

1. The Three-Way Passage carrying Boston rum to Africa, slaves to America (mostly to South America and Caribbean), and molasses back to Boston—a profit on each leg of the passage.

2. The European carrying trade, a New England monopoly, granted by the long-lasting Anglo-French wars.

3. Capital transferred to manufacturing during the Embargo and War of 1812.

The slave trade became illegal for Americans in 1808, and the wars ended by 1815. Those monopolies were finished. The cotton gin had come to their rescue, providing all the cotton from the South that the New England mills could use. The merchants turned from the sea to the mill. Accustomed to monopolies, New England money men wanted another one to take their place—a captive market for their manufactures and a source of cheap raw materials. To get it, they looked South.

The South continued agricultural. An agricultural land of vast size and few people cannot easily establish a manufacturing, banking, and commercial economy. Especially when there is such a powerful one flourishing in the same country. The New England merchants had accumulated wealth so vast that the Southerner even today cannot conceive of what the Bostonians had and have. People in each section did what was natural for their local circumstances. Those circumstances made them increasingly different, but that did not make a war.

As colonists in the New World they were different because of their different soil, climate, culture, and economy. Sectional differences increased after the colonies became states. The North, of thin soil, small area, and large population condensed into towns, became more and more industrial. Three monopolies accumulated great capital, and they became a banking and finance power. Falling waters gave them water power, urban population gave them labor and market for manufacturing. The South, of small population spread over a vast area of fertile land, remained agricultural. Those differences had not necessitated war before and did not necessitate it in 1861.

Agriculture and commerce are opposites. Antagonists. World history is the story of a powerful commercial economy devouring a weaker agricultural.

Another difference was the system of labor. In colonial days many people bought passage to America by selling the right of ownership in their labor. Called an indenture, it was the old master-apprentice system in Europe, usually set for a period. A man, Anthony Johnson, in 1653 petitioned the Northampton County, Virginia, court for a lifetime indenture, an ownership of labor, not of life, person, or body. The system of temporary indentured servants of colonial days had given way to the system of slavery. One of the American colonies] first slaveowners, Anthony Johnson, was black.

At first the North extolled slavery for its improvement in the material and spiritual condition of the black people they were bringing over. There were slaves in every American colony as well as throughout the Caribbean and South America. The North gradually sold their slaves South. The Northern states enacted statutes assisting sale of slaves over extended periods, gradually phasing out an institution of no use to them. A twenty-year time period gave ample opportunity to sell them at a profit.

In the South the original English population had been slowly broadened by meeting French and by adding Scots, Irish, Scots-Irish, Negroes, Germans, Dutch, Huguenots, and a few Sephardic Jews. All those peoples fused into a unitary society, unknown in and incomprehensible to the North. Increments were assimilated.

The South featured a social structure outsiders cannot understand. As different as they seemed from a distance, their common farming base and stable culture made their society unitary. Black and white were closer there than white and white in Boston, a condition incomprehensible to Boston. Boston had 250,000 people when Richmond had 15,000. Colored and white in the South were close, spatially and sentimentally. The Bostonians were estranged from the mill workers and never developed with their domestic servants the “family” relationship of the South. City businessmen are rivals; farm folks, slave or non-slave, are mutually dependent.

In the South, even the towns were rural in affiliation. Southerners black and white lived and ate and slept and worked close together. They went to the same church. Farmers are more intimate and more equal than city folks, especially city folks with little in common. The South had a whole life in common. The races in the South had close lives.

Mrs. Benjamin Williams found this out and wrote it in her letters. Mrs. Williams, married in her native Abolitionist upstate New York, traveled with her husband to his North Carolina home. Leaving the railroad in Wilson, they rode in a buggy to her husband’s Greene County plantation. She was surprised to see slaves, not her husband’s slaves, all along the way, running up to welcome, obviously glad to see them. Twenty miles away they knew each other. They arrived (as did Thomas Jefferson, with his new bride) during the night when nobody was about. The next morning, lying in bed with her husband, she was astonished when two little slave girls came running into the room to welcome her to their home.

The North could not understand the South. And mostly did not want to. Tocqueville said the white Southerners liked the Negro, and vice versa, that the white Northerners disliked the Negro, the dislike increasing the farther one went into Abolitionist territory. There were wide differences between the two sections in social circumstances, in religion, in philosophy of life. The South had a life that only a rare Yankee could understand, and no Jacobin would. The South was a harmonious Christian society. After the war Northern writers who went South found there indeed a different place. They reported a different culture, a Christian-based society of higher values. They used such adjectives as "gentility, manners, generosity, honesty." Henry James called it "nobility."

While the South was a unit, the North in the later antebellum period was flooded with so many immigrants that they could not be assimilated. Northern cities became foreign places, their society heterogeneous. The immigrants were perfectly ignorant of the South, and of the North too. Numerous, they were a political and social different thing. They brought European class conflict and revolutionary ideology. Different varieties of people brought different varieties of philosophy and prejudice. Northern people lived condensed in cities but strangers to each other. Southern folks lived wider spaced, but in closer intimacy as individuals.

Not only were the New Englanders different from the South, they were becoming increasingly different from one another; the Yankee had become different from himself. They were estranged from their own background. Descended from Bible-believing, strict Calvinists, the social, economic, and intellectual leaders of New England went to the opposite pole of philosophy. In less than a generation the Boston intelligentsia departed from hundreds of years of their own culture. Harvard College, established for religion, threw it out, becoming Unitarian in 1805. That began a radical departure from the South, a real sectional difference. A radical difference from its own self rapidly moved thought into revolt. The descendants of the Puritans rebelled against Calvinism, descended into Humanism. The Christian Gospel of love gave way to the Socialist doctrine of hate.

The North was agitated by people of the air, those who live by theories and fantasies. Humanism produced dissension. Heterogeneous peoples and heterogeneous philosophies produced an agitated society. In the South, humanism never took root. People were tied to the soil, grounded in reality, not floating on airy speculation and fantasy. The discord of the North was absent in the South. The South was quiet and peaceful. Paradox though it seems, the South, containing two distinct races, was a unitary society. Rural or in small town, black and white lived together, worked together, ate dinner together, went to church together, were mutually dependent, prospered or failed together, and suffered together. The same doctor tended them both.

Richard Weaver called the South the last non-materialist civilization in the West and the only civilization where all classes of society subscribed to the values of the aristocrat. Virtue was their standard. White and black, rich and poor, embraced the same set of values. Their leaders were farmers, not money men; their society was not based on money but on family, manners, and character. Their farmer-magistrates were chosen for their virtue, and their people aspired to it. This is not to say that they attained virtue, but they were oriented by it. They lived in quiet harmony. A rural society, living with nature, made the people content to live with God. They remained unchanged, and even to the present day the most religious part of the nation. Even then, Europeans said of America, "The Yankees live for getting and having, The Southerners live for being." The South continued in the even tenor of its ways.

Sectional difference was not the cause of the war. It was merely background. Background is the stage on which the actors move. Background is not battlefield. It is the actors who draw the sword. Where people have differing interests they will always have contention. Differences can be discussed without war. It is one thing to dispute. It is quite another thing to conceive, plan, and order up a massive, burning, death-dealing war. Contention is not war, it is only an excuse for war. War—the worst terror.

Forget all the North-South differences but one—MONEY. The economies of the North and South were "different and antagonistic." New England was ruled by the commerce party: bankers, merchants, mill owners. "The union must be preserved" was the slogan of the money men only. The war was made by the greed of a party and power lust of a politician. A politician made war for power and for private interests. History has not yet apprehended his false description of the beginning of the war: "And the war came." The war did not "come," and it did not "come" from "sectional differences." It was brought, made, by a man and his party. War did not just appear: a man went to considerable thought and put others to considerable effort to bring it.

Despite all the differences, the ordinary folks, North and South, were getting along quite well with each other. They had no quarrel. The ordinary citizen had no thought, no desire, to fight a war with the other section. None.

The Red Herring "Slavery"

"There is very little moral mixture in the 'antislavery' feeling in this country. A great deal is abstract philanthropy, part is jealousy for white labor, part is hatred of white slave-holders. How we hate those we injure. I can say so, being 'anti-slavery,' myself."

—GEORGE W. CURTIS, EDITOR, PUBLISHER, HARPER'S WEEKLY, PRIVATE LETTER, JULY 29, 1861

"The Northern onslaught upon slavery was no more than a piece of specious humbug designed to conceal its desire for economic control of the Southern states."

—CHARLES DICKENS, 1862

Ohio Abolitionist Congressman Joshua Giddings reveals the real reason he opposes "Slavery" entering new states: "To give the South the preponderance of political power will be itself a surrender of our Tariff, our internal improvements, our distribution of proceeds of public lands."

"Two hundred Negroes in Petersburg today offered themselves 'for any work needed: to fight, dig ditches, do anything to serve Old Virginia.'"

—RICHMOND DISPATCH, APRIL 1861

A RED HERRING is a fish used in training hounds, dragged across the track to distract, to confuse, to make their task harder. In debate it is the trick of diverting attention from the real question at hand by throwing in an irrelevant but exciting subject.

Today's history books cite the "slavery issue" as the dominant regional difference before the war and the cause of the war. It was not the determining issue of the conflict. The money party raised it before the war to cover their policy and after the war to justify their making it and their savagery in waging it.

Like "Union" the term "slavery" has a fictional life and fictional personality of its own. It is thought of not as a fact but in the abstract, as a metaphysical character, not what it really was. Regimented by Political Correctness, contemporary professional historians present a false image. Popular opinion has been shaped as: "There was slavery before the war, none after. How good the war."

Slaves were not an abused people straining to be free. The true nature of slavery is not just a corporate name of evil, it is a subject that concerned four million individual slaves, a million free blacks, and five million white people. They were, each of them, individuals who struggled with enough of life's problems before a selfish few politicians forced upon them cruel, unnecessary war. The cure was far worse than the disease.

They all suffered together from that war. The Southern people, slaves included, were far better off before the war. The whole country was better off without the war. Slavery had no part in Lincoln's decision to make war. Black Southerners, slave and free, were more loyal to the South during the war than were the whites in the North to Lincoln. Many blacks were more loyal to the Confederacy than some whites in the South. Lincoln's Republicans spent much money and great effort to entice the black people of the South to revolt. The project elicited little response. Republicans were disappointed.

There were more slave traders in Africa than America. The institution of slavery was of ancient lineage. For hundreds of years the system of one man owning the labor of another was universal over the world. In Britain a man who wanted to go to Virginia but lacked the money could gain passage by granting his labor to the ownership of another. It was called an "indenture." That system was used by many to get to the New World. At the end of the indenture he could go out on his own.

A second form was established in 1653. Anthony Johnson, a black man, sued in the court in Northampton County, Virginia Colony, for right to permanent ownership of the labor of one John Casor. The court decided that Casor was better off under Johnson's care than on his own and granted Johnson property rights in the labor of Casor. Anthony Johnson became one of the first slave owners in the American colonies.

Robert Beverley of Virginia, visiting in London, saw a book on his colony. The book was so full of errors that Beverley, believing Virginia deserved description by someone who had actually seen it, wrote one, *The History and Present State of Virginia* (1715). He gave its real conditions of life, proving that the treatment of the slaves in North America was quite good. Beverly said the slaves were better nurtured than the indentured because they were less able to care for themselves and owners had so much invested in them. He invited the English to go see for themselves. All libraries have Beverley's fascinating book. William Byrd's diary, of the same time, tells the benign nature of slavery, and entertains. That was the institution of slavery. Like all man's works it was imperfect, but the real institution was far different from the false "issue."

No one, North or South, thought they were injuring the slaves, rather the contrary. The Negroes, captives of tribal war, were already slaves in Africa, and would have fared worse if left there. One impressive evidence, confirmed during the next century and a half, was the improved health, life span, and prodigious fecundity of the Negroes in America compared to Africa. The New England divines waxed eloquent and correctly that the slaves were better off in America, much advanced in material and spiritual condition.

In 1853, Sarah Frances Hicks, the abolitionist from upstate New York who had married Benjamin Williams and traveled to his home in Greene County, North Carolina, was astonished to learn that both races considered themselves family, called each other family, and functioned as family. They were truly intimate, lived in an affection not seen with white peers of the one race in the North.

The true relation startled her, so different from the Abolitionist propaganda she had known. She wrote home that the Northern people did not live on such personal terms with their white servants.

Without too much difficulty, any slave who wanted to go North could get on a train and go. Very few did and they generally faced an uncertain reception in the North and would likely end up in Canada. Fugitives never made up more than 1% of the slave population. Black people did not leave the South in any significant numbers until well into the 20th century, and then only from economic necessity. They are now returning.

Slave testimony taken by U.S. Government in the 1930s revealed that they regarded slavery days as far better than afterward.

Recent studies like Fogel and Engerman's *Time on the Cross* indicate that the slaves enjoyed a better life than many "free" workers in the North and Europe. The Lincoln and Grant families were both involved in and profited from slave ownership without feeling any loss of respectability.

***

The "slavery issue" had little to do the realities of life in the South. "Slavery" was intruded into the regional quarrel between North and South by a political party as a red herring to mask their thirst for public money. The real regional quarrel was money.

In 1776 the colonies seceded from England. Thirteen separate colonies became thirteen independent and sovereign states. To conduct certain specific common functions they formed a "general" or "federal" government. State rights was and is the method by which a federal system maintains freedom, government by the people instead of by the ruler. The states wrote twice in each of two successive constitutions that the central or common government had only certain delegated powers, that the powers not given it were retained by the states or the private citizens. They called their union of states the "Confederacy" until 1860. The states were sovereign, the Federal Government had only the powers that the states granted it. But, the states made a fatal error: they failed to build in a counter power to oppose the central power. They did not sufficiently anticipate the selfishness of the faction that would control the central government. Only power can oppose power.

To pay the expenses of the central government the states gave Congress in the Constitution the power to tax goods imported from foreign countries, an already familiar tax called custom duty or tariff. It was a revenue tax only, a tax for one purpose—to raise money, "revenue," to support the central government. The tariff mainly took from those who were well off enough to buy imported goods.

The interests of the Northern and Southern states were different. Geographic differences made the North leave agriculture for business and the South remain agricultural. Since Greece and Rome commerce and agriculture have fought; the city or money party always dominates and eventually parasitizes the farmers. The South lived by foreign trade—exchanging their farm and forest products for European manufactures. The North lived by financial, merchant, and manufacturing business. Doing little foreign trade, they paid little tax. The South paid the tax. It was not fair or legal, the Constitution mandated equal taxes, but in a spirit of good will the South agreed to it. The first tariffs were low—5 to 10 percent.

Many framers of the Constitution wanted a two-thirds rather than a simple majority to pass a tariff law, but the final document required only a majority vote. The South objected: Patrick Henry, John Tyler Sr., and Charles Pinckney predicted that the North's growing population advantage would give control of Congress to the Northern money party (later embodied as Federalist, Whig, Republican), who would enact tariff increases and other measures forcing the South to subsidize them. George Mason warned: "The terms of this contract will deliver the Southern farmer, bound and tied, to the New England merchants." He begged the South not to agree to the Constitution as proposed; he refused to sign the document he largely wrote. If five votes in the Virginia and North Carolina conventions had switched, those states would not have ratified, other states would have seen the threat, and the North would have compromised, preventing all the later horrors.

Southern prophecy was confirmed. Congress did enact North favoring measures, did change the tariff from a "revenue" tariff to a "protective" tariff to subsidize Northern factory owners and investors. The South paid the tax; the North spent it and raised it about every five years. Raising tariffs raised the price of European goods, reduced the price of Southern goods, blocked the South's efficient 200-year trade with Europe, gave the North a captive market, forced the South to buy from a Northern monopoly who set their own prices for their products.

The South, poorer in money, smaller in population, paid five-sixths of the taxes. Prosperous as colonies, the South became depressed as states. Senator Thomas H. Benton spoke: "The South used to be the seat of wealth and hospitality; all that is left now is the hospitality." Government action injured farming, the nation's most valuable industry. The North hurt the South far more than England hurt the colonies.

The money quarrel was first about tariff, who paid it and who spent it and what for. Taxes were supposed to be uniform, but the South paid it and the North spent it. Then it got worse. The North began spending it to benefit private interests. It was unconstitutional. That did not deter them.

The tariff depressed the Southern economy and enriched the Northern rich. The abuse grew as the Northern majority grew. The money party had no valid justification for their demands, and no attractive features. Lacking personal virtue and patriotism of their own, they found sin in their opponent. They found the "slavery issue." "Miss Slavery," destined to become a servant of the money party, was not called up until they needed to throw her apron over their tariff monster.

The money party piggybacked on the Abolitionists who preached to the North for thirty years before the war that Southerners were an evil, depraved, barbarous people who were an obstacle to bringing on the true America—which looked a lot like New England.

The institution of slavery was irrelevant to the real regional quarrel—the Northern capitalists' greed and the Northern politician's desire for power. The 1829-32 quarrel with South Carolina was wholly tariff. The Northern politicians threw "slavery" at that small state; historians have continued to do so. The industrial/financial party could not win elections, even in the North, on their profit-seeking agenda. So they adopted the standard procedure of politicians to make an "issue," to seek power by alarming the electorate with a false "peril" from which the politicians will "save" them.

They alarmed the North, especially the ignorant immigrants, with the false cry that "slavery" was a danger to them, that the Southern farmers, if allowed to come North, would bring Negroes with them, would even enslave immigrants.

The money party wanted to keep the South out of new territories because a farm state would vote against taxing farmers to subsidize Northern industry. Lincoln's "anti-slavery" was really "Anti-Negro," dishonestly making a false alarm, stimulating anti-Negro fear. Five hundred or a thousand miles away, Northerners did not care for the slaves personally as people or for the truth of the institution: all they cared about was the "issue" for their issue-less party. Slavery was coincidental and happened to be in only one region. So the politicians could safely use it in the other region. It was a perfect device. If the South had been agricultural but without slaves they would have invented another "difference," another red herring.

The real argument was MONEY—Southern taxes subsidizing Northern business—and POWER—party control of Federal Government. The South asked for nothing more than what they had at the beginning—fair treatment in taxation and the fair right to move into new territories. The anti-South faction began to insult Southern character. That faction took office. Lincoln promised his party's high tariff, North-favoring, South-injuring program. At last, the South fled. Seven states seceded, declared independence for the same but stronger reason as the colonies—exploitation by hostile outside power.

Abraham Lincoln's new government set the highest tariffs in the world—60% on some articles. The Confederate States set a tariff of 5% to 10%—the principle of free trade. Goods imported into Southern ports would be much cheaper than those coming into Northern. Trade would leave the North, go South. The South would no longer be paying the tariff that had subsidized the Northern money men, paid their taxes, paid for their "internal improvements." The captive South would have escaped their captors. The Northern rich for the first time would have to pay taxes and spend their own money on their public works.

Jefferson Davis, whom Republican William H. Seward more esteemed than he did Lincoln, said: "We seek nothing from the States with which we were lately confederated. All we ask is to be let alone; we ask only that those who never had power over us will not now attempt to subjugate us by war." The day after the Confederate Congress set its tariff Lincoln's party newspapers and politicians demanded war to prevent Southern independence. Lincoln knew that it is illegal for a president to make war, only Congress has that power; he said so in 1848. But in peace his party would be ejected at the next election. War was the only way they could keep possession of the Federal offices. No man had the legal power to make war but one man had the physical power. It would be illegal, but he could give the orders. Lincoln set his war. America's bloodiest. The blood is on his hands.

***

John Tyler and James Knox Polk. Two of America's best presidents. What did they have to do with the "slavery issue"? Nothing.

Tyler, president from 1841 to 1845, said he hoped not a single significant piece of legislation would pass while he was in office, the government being already too big. He tried to run a modest, frugal government. The Northern Whigs hated Tyler for vetoing their money bills. Polk, president from 1845 to 1849, also believed in limited government, promised seven goals, promised to do no more. He attained the seven, did no more—the only president ever to do such. The money party opposed Polk and Texas because he was, and Texas was expected to be, for free trade and frugal government. The Northern attack on the two presidents proves the real motive: subsidizing itself with government money, not helping or freeing the slaves.

The money party used the red herring of "slavery" to confuse, first the tariff, then territory, then elections. They injected "slavery" into any regional difference to divert attention from the real disagreements. When the South complained of the latest abuse the money party would not respond to the question but start hurling insults about "immoral slavery."

"Slavery" was a campaign tool to confound the real quarrel, to make a party seem to have some concern besides itself, to weaken the opposite party, to taint the Democrats, to frighten the voters, to polarize the nation, to win elections, to gain power. "Slavery" had everything to do with the election of 1860.

Slavery had nothing to do with the war of 1861. Once elected and "slavery" no longer of use, Lincoln discarded the issue and promised to protect slavery. He offered the South every assurance of protection, several times promised the preservation of slavery if the seceded states would return. The South refused to return. Their grievance was not slavery but threatening and exploitive outside power. The North's was loss of money. Slavery was not why the South seceded. Slavery was not why the North made war.

Abraham Lincoln did not start war to stop slavery. His words and deeds made that clear enough. In 1861 nobody thought or mentioned slavery as cause of war. The North did not fight for freedom, they fought to prevent freedom. Secession was why the Republicans made war. The South seceded to escape. Lincoln and his Congress gave the official reasons for war. Slavery was not one of them. "Slavery" disappeared for two years. Then, it was fabricated again to save the Republican Party's failing war of usurpation. The Emancipation Proclamation, another fraud, was a military and political move.

To hide their greed Lincoln's party kept 19th century America in turmoil, drumming the false "slavery issue." Then, threatened with loss of their victim, to insult they added the worst of injuries—killing, war. They threw the disguise of "slavery" over that crime, too. It is not charity that makes violence. They violated all the American people, even to this day, though New England has not yet realized it.

There was no economic use for slavery in the North. Slaves there were gradually sold off, a far smaller proportion freed than the Southerners freed. In 1860 there were more free black people in the South than in the North. The North never lost any money from emancipation. Slavery was gradually terminating over the world, and it would have done so in the South.

For more than forty years those selfish, ambitious men prevented their country from attending to its real needs. Surely the United States had matters that really concerned the welfare of the country, matters of substance that were thrown aside by those unprincipled men. That was guilt enough, but their war was far worse—America's premier crime. The Abolitionists made the background, but the politicians made the battleground.

The South was not destroyed to destroy slavery. "Slavery" was an excuse to destroy the South. The "slavery issue" was a weapon to destroy the Democratic Party, the obstacle to Republican Party power. The "slavery issue" was as false as "Union." Low politicians invented the "slavery issue" to raise themselves, used it again to excuse a war, fastened it so tight upon America's polity that it confounds public life still, seven score years later.

"The commercial and manufacturing States will dominate and make the Southern States their milk cow whose substance the North will extract."

—WILLIAM GRAYSON, FIRST SENATOR FROM VIRGINIA, 1789

"The Party of Lincoln attacked the South militarily to prevent escape of the victim they had abused economically and politically for so long... The slavery issue was no more than harassment to divert from the real aim."

—RAPHAEL SEMMES

Abolition

"They were such a variety of queer, strangely-dressed, oddly-behaved mortals, who took upon themselves to be important agents of the world's destiny, yet were simply bores of a very intense water. Their triteness of novelty is enough to make any man of common sense blaspheme at all ideas of less than a century's standing, and pray that the world may be petrified and rendered fixed immoveable in the worst moral and physical state it ever arrived at rather than be benefited by such schemes of such philosophers."

—NATHANIEL HAWTHORNE ON NEW ENGLAND REFORMERS

"The sole purpose of the Abolitionists is to array one portion of the Union against the other. The alleged horrors of slavery are depicted in exaggerated colors to stimulate the rage of the people of the non-slave states against the people of the South. Why are the Southern people so cruelly and so wickedly assailed? Why does the Abolitionist press excite hatred and animosity against the South?

—HENRY CLAY

NORTHERN PHILOSOPHY was speculation, dreams by men of the air. Southern philosophy was of the soil—reality. Northern abstractions were put to concrete use by men of the world who speculated only in money and power. Southern thought contained no idea of intruding upon the lives of others far away.

Different and antagonistic in industry for reasons due to nature, the people of the North and South soon became different and antagonistic in philosophy due to nurture. The Boston intellectuals began nursing revolution. Revolution—the creed of the intellectual. Nobody but an intellectual would be stupid enough to love the French Revolution. They took seeds from the Enlightenment and French Revolution and cultivated in their drawing rooms a noisome plant—Humanism. Humanism, the claimed religion of the Radical or Jacobin—or "Liberal."

In colonial New England, intellectual leadership had been vested in the Calvinist preachers. By 1800 that strict, severe religion had left their grandchildren, or rather they left it. Wealthy Boston could afford a class of people who did not have to work, the idle affluent, the "intellectuals." In 1805, Harvard College renounced Christianity and joined the Unitarian club. Those radicals, ("liberals" today) expelled their religion, and then of course, looked around for something to take its place. When man loses his belief in God he will believe everything and anything. The sin of the idle educated.

The New England leaders of thought supplanted religion with philosophy. And from that attempt to have man and God switch places came ideas, theories, fantasies, projects, worse still—movements—by which man would change the world, not in the only way he can, by changing himself, but by forcing change on others. That operation is called wrong by Christianity and proven impossible by history. Humanism's children were Romanticism, Rousseauism, Positivism, Relativism, Secularism, Atheism, Unitarianism, Universalism, Deism, Pantheism, Modernism, Socialism, Communism. Idealism usurped the place of faith. Idealism is a false religion, an expression of human egotism, pride, and vanity. And impotence. The rhetoric of idealism cannot bring on the perfect state. The talk grows more elegant as the world stumbles from one disaster to another. And disaster is what those people delivered.

The world of the flesh and the Devil does not like God's command that the only way man can change the world is to change himself. The Devil offers to change the world by the easier means of correcting others, doubly attractive as it relieves self and afflicts others. Truly, the Devil's Proposition. The first fruit of this Enlightenment was the terror of the French Revolution. Later crops were the North's war on the South and the violence of the 20th century.

The descendants of the New England Puritans, no longer burning witches, began to blister the slaveholder. They were going to improve the world by assaulting another "evil." But there was more to what they were about than just theory and idealism. Everybody, North and South, was against slavery, but there was a realistic side of it. The South had its money and life tied up in it. Instant abolishment of slavery, sudden destruction of four billions of capital, the sudden throwing into the world of four million dependents, would ruin the whole South, everybody, slave and master, and non-slaves too, white and black. Left alone, slavery would have gradually and quietly played out, with minimum distress. The Southern farmer's capital was not money but land and slaves. Take suddenly the capital out of any economy and the result is ruin.

But, the intellectuals who had thrown away their religion would gain earthly power by taking up (not "on") the sins of other people. They had found a substitute for religion—a "moral issue."

"Intellectual" does not mean "intelligent." Hippolyte Taine, the French historian, said that intellectuals, for no good reason, will suddenly take up a foolish notion, which becomes fashionable, however absurd or vicious. He termed it the "*Grande Idee*," a Grand Idea, entering the mind of the idle vain who prefer theory to reality. And a distant revolution to a personal act of charity at home. They preached "equality" to Haiti. The slaves killed every white person on the island—thirty thousand. "Abolition," fashion for the idle, became a righteous role for the Gospel-leaving New England clergy. By other names ("Civil Rights") it is still here. Agitation by a faction to gain power.

In the late 1700s European drawing-room intellectuals took on schemes to change the world: property in common, the all-powerful state (socialism), the cry of "equality." "Equality" ruled the drawing rooms, and then the tavern, enlarged itself to include all creation. One fact is certain: mankind are not equal, and never will be. After "equality" came the inevitable sequel—inequality, the declaration of Jean Jacques Rousseau that the civilized were inferior to the savage. Astonishingly, his imbecility was endorsed. He was a flighty parasite, insane, but had great influence upon the intellectuals with his notion that savage man is superior to civilized man. The nonworking upper classes spread that doctrine. The idea of the "Noble Savage" still appeals to the leftists, to man's base nature. It appeals to the selfish envy of all us sinners.

Alexis de Tocqueville saw this popular madness in America. In a "Democracy" false notions become "correct thinking" and woe to the one who dares think different. He said there is more free speech in Europe because the aristocracy dares to object to popular fashion. In America mass opinion will deliver swift punishment to the eccentric who objects to folly. Today in America one who violates thought control will not be imprisoned but he will live the rest of his life derided, deprived of civil liberties, denied employment, and refused public office. At the end of the 20th century, Solzhenitsyn described America: "There is no official government censorship in the United States but all the press say exactly the same thing." It is given the kind name "Political Correctness" which veils the fact that force is involved. There is much truth that cannot be uttered in the United States at the beginning of the third millennium. Truth is not now allowed in public discourse. A false conception of life, a fantasy, an avoidance of reality issues from the artificial havens of the idle, educated affluent, causes more damage than the man on horseback.

Humanism is as good a name as any to call it.

Socialism was one poisonous fruit from the tree of Humanism. Two great thinkers were able to see the moral and intellectual falsity of these "Grand Ideas." In the South it was John Randolph of Roanoke, who in 1829 said of socialism:

"Among the strange notions that have been broached since I have been in the political theater, there is one that has lately seized the minds of men. It is that all things are to be done for them by the government, that they are to do nothing for themselves. The government, in addition to its great concerns, its proper province, must step into the life of the individual, and relieve him of his moral and natural obligations. No more pernicious doctrine could prevail. Given time, this will produce a nation where you will find the father emerging unsteadily from a whiskey shop, the mother a slattern walking the street, and the children ragged and dirty, neglected, running wild, fit candidates for prison. Ask the parents why this is so and they will answer, 'Oh, the government is going to educate our children and care for us.'"

A few in the North, like Hawthorne, saw through Humanism. That he saw the falsity of Humanism when it ruled the North is a tribute to his genius in recognizing and courage in resisting the madness that laid hold of his fellow intellectuals. No Southerner better saw the evil in the New England philosophy. But Hawthorne was wrong in believing they would have no influence on the real world. Those vain bores "took upon themselves to be important agents of the world's destiny." Although they were few in number, and were, even in Boston, by most people either ignored or disdained, although regarded as harmless zealots, their belief in their importance did come to pass. They did a lot of harm. It was they whose agitation gave the politicians an issue, a tool, for ambition to employ and make a war. That awful consequence was foretold when Abraham Lincoln met William Seward, and said, "It is time we look into this slavery thing." That is, what use can we put it to, what can it do for us.

That was the intellectual background. From it was produced a corrupt philosophy. From that philosophy came issues which ambitious politicians used to break open the door to power. The doctrine of those philosophers was false and malignant, old as the Bible, and reappears with every generation. It begins as man's desire to be God. Given power he will do the Devil's work. Its error has been exposed by Russell Kirk in the 20th century, by Hawthorne in the 19th, and by Edmund Burke in the 18th.

The Humanist movement made "Abolition." "Abolition" made an issue. An issue made a constituency. A constituency made a politician. And a politician made a war. The issue was fabricated. The politicians cared not that the issue was fake—it served their purpose. The philosophy, the issue, did not cause the war, it gave the politicians an excuse for war. Slavery did not cause secession, but abolition did. Its untiring and venomous abuse alarmed the South.

A philosophical difference can be discussed, an economic difference can be tolerated. Even the fulmination of the self-righteous, narrow, hypocritical, drawing-room intellectuals has limited power to do evil. But, when people looking to profit by the difference, the money men seeking money and the politicians seeking power, get hold of it, that is politics. And trouble.

They were ignorant of each other. They were thus susceptible to false information and victims of selfish leaders. The ordinary citizens in the North and South had no enmity for one another, certainly no desire to kill each other. The intellectual background came into contact with the economic background and political background of the North. The money party had little intellectual background. They had an agenda.

Everybody opposed slavery. What to do? Before the American Revolution "abolition" did not appeal to Boston. They were busy making money off the slave trade. Abolition" means abolishing, doing away with something. Catherine the Great abolished state intervention into commerce. Good result. Lenin abolished private commerce. Bad result. In 19th century history it referred to abolishing slavery. "Abolition" seems an honest word, a goal desired by all.

North America was settled at Jamestown in 1607. Many of the early settlers came as temporary slaves, that is, they obtained their passage money by signing over their labor to another person, for whom they worked. It was the centuries-old, master-apprentice labor system. American slavery meant owning the labor of another, not his body. It never was slavery in a brutal sense, it was domestic servitude, a mutual service and dependency.

In 1619 a ship landed at Jamestown with 20 Negroes. They were not made slaves. In 1653 Anthony Johnson asked the Northampton court to grant him the right of permanent ownership in the labor of one John Casor. The court granted Johnson's petition. By 1700 there were slaves in all the colonies.

For more than a century there was no defense made of the institution of slavery because there was no attack on it. In the first hundred years, from about 1700 to 1800, the world paid little attention to slavery. Many of the slaves were brought over by New Englanders, not by the South. At least 94% of the slaves went to South America and the Caribbean. In North America they were mostly brought from 1700 until transport ended in 1808. The numbers were about 3,500 a year. The total number was less than 500,000.

From 1709 forward the Virginia Government petitioned to abolish slave imports, but was overruled by London and Boston power. All people realized that slavery, and a race so numerous, so different, and so primitive, was a problem and slated to become a worse problem. Men of good will began to talk of ending slavery and of repatriation back to Africa, putting them back in their own "patria" (country). Abolition of slavery appealed to all people. It was discussed in a civil manner. In every state societies were formed to search ways to free and repatriate them.

A few decades after the Revolution the new thinking appeared in Boston. But not until they had lost their monopolies: the slave trade in 1808, war trade and carrying trade in 1815. Boston demanded and was granted tariff and other monopolies. Boston soon took up "slavery." Two factors propelled it:

1. A "*Grande Idee*," imported from Europe.

2. A red herring to divert attention from their tariff robbery.

Boston intellectuals rejected their Puritan religion in favor of Unitarianism but had not rejected the Puritan's love to punish others. The Abolitionists were theorizing zealots, intellectuals in an area where there were no slaves, almost no Negroes. It was a safe subject for them, posing no threat to their own well-being. Abolition was part of a radical, a so-called "reform," movement (reform everybody but themselves).

Abolitionists came to notice in America about 1830. "Abolition" no longer meant people of good will who opposed slavery, but became a proper noun; the word "Abolitionist" came to be spelled with a capital letter, making it not just a word but a proper name of a particular party. "Abolition" gave those revolutionaries an issue of broader appeal. They sought power, and here was a subject that appealed to the good will of normal people. What they had in mind was not to abolish slavery in some decent and feasible manner. It was not a moral political movement, but a revolutionary one. "Abolition" came to mean not just the desire to accomplish a good end, but a means to power, a good word masking an evil nature, selfish purpose, and destructive result. They became an aggressive, organized, wealthy party.

The Abolitionists labeled the owner class as villains, the slave class as abject sufferers. They were revolutionaries, found any time where people have sufficient exemption from bread-winning and insufficient control of the desire to control others. They became a mixed party, zealots attracting innocents. They were upper class. Abolitionists never numbered many; it was said in Boston that if one bus load were run out of town the whole Abolition movement would collapse. But there was a string of them that extended across New England, the Northern tier of counties in New York, Ohio, and over as far as Iowa. By themselves they would have done little harm. The trouble was, they would not stay by themselves. They were politicians, they joined other politicians.

At first the Abolitionists had little power. Most people in Boston regarded them as idle trouble makers. They were ignored by the politicians. Both parties disdained them, a handicap to a politician. Then, they became so loud, the politicians lacked nerve to reject them—to oppose them would seem to be endorsing slavery. They began to make the politicians uncomfortable, both parties fearing to be labeled "pro-slavery." With each concession the Abolitionists demanded more. Having once scorned them, the Northern money party politicians began to court their favor. They saw the obvious: "slavery" was a perfect weapon to injure the rival farmer party. It was like a newly-discovered weapon of war, a weapon not possessed by the other side. Over two generations slavery had gradually faded away in the North.

The money party became Abolitionists. The money party began to submit anti-slavery petitions to Congress, attaching anti-slavery laws to every bill, using "slavery" as excuse to cover their money bills and to block the Southern party out of new states. John

Quincy Adams, forced out of the executive office by the Democrats, served in Congress for twenty years thereafter, his hatred of the South never cooled. He used his power to offend the South with every possible use of "slavery."

The agitation of the politicians had evil effect on personal life.

Years before the War, the Northern Methodist Church expelled the Southern Methodists. For ninety years the Methodist Church, South, was a separate body. Which side was the sinner? The Methodist bishops continue yet today their practice of joining fashionable political, secular movements, even Communist, anti-Christian, described in great good humor by the born-Methodist Malcolm Muggeridge.

The Abolition movement was not benign as many, many people in the North realized. It was Jacobin, aimed against "sin," to destroy the slaveholder rather than to help the slave. Abolition was supposed to liberate the slaves. It chained them to ruin. The results of its work were injurious to everybody.

The original opposition to slavery was sincere and universal. At first the money men and the Abolitionists were two distinct groups, but mutual reward blurred the distinction. The money party was in it for money. The Emigrant Aid Society in Kansas was presented as a scheme to make money by making strife in Kansas.

The Abolitionists were radicals, leftists. Today they call themselves "Democrats," and "liberals," but are in fact Jacobins and Socialists. Their relation to life persists today. Their philosophy flies in the face of sense and charity, and has long since been discredited. But it is still widespread among politicians, college professors, and others of the subsidized classes. They believe it serves their interest. Stirring class hate will never die because it is a means to power. The Abolitionists provided the professional politicians a tool. The politicians saw they could use the Abolitionists to get at the Democrats. It happened that the party they hated was almost as much a part of the South as the Whigs were of Boston. Indict "slavery," kill the Democrats. It was obvious. Abraham Lincoln, on a trip East, talked to Senator Seward. He spoke these ominous words: "I reckon it is time we looked into this slavery thing." That is, look for what good we can get out of it. When it was of use to him, as Herndon said, "He became our abolition leader."

Of course the people in the Northeast were opposed to slavery. Everybody opposed it in principle. For the Abolitionists slavery was only a concept. Bringing the slaves to America had brought fortunes to the richest people in New England. To the North it had brought wealth but not black people. The black people were elsewhere; they were not going to move to New England. Slavery was a distant affair, a theoretical toy to play with.

For the South, both black and white, it was different. The South had to live with everyday facts. The South had little money. Their capital was tied up in land and labor. Sudden abolishment of slavery would wreak catastrophe. It would destroy Southern capital and welfare of everybody. Why should they be forced to do it, the North had not done it. The North had lost no money by ending slavery.

Lincoln made a war. Not to end slavery; he said so himself. He made war for the reason of all wars—money, and the only thing worse than money—power. Slavery was not the cause of the eighty-year North-South argument—it was money. Lincoln offered twice to add to the Constitution a second guarantee of slavery if the states would return—none did. Slavery was not why Lincoln made war. Europe and the informed North knew why Lincoln made war—party usurpation, to prevent loss of Southern money and the Federal executive office.

Lincoln's immoral war of usurpation wears a moral dress bought by an evil act. In 1862 the Republican Party suffered military defeat, election defeat, recruiting failure, soldier disaffection, public disfavor, and a Northern peace movement. The party expected their downfall. "Party" was not the 39% who voted Republican. "Party" is not the individuals, the people on the outside who cast a vote for a stranger. "Party" really means the inside elite who direct and profit by it. In December battle defeats added the prospect of imminent public rejection. Christmas Eve was a nightmare for the Republican Party. They were sore afraid. But, they had a savior.

Lincoln's Springfield friends said that "he had no industry, no knowledge, no judgment, no business." "All he knew was politics. He was lazy, avoided work, spoiled his children." But on Christmas Eve Lincoln got busy and forgot his children. That night he induced the passive Burnside to take Lincoln's blame for Fredericksburg. He and his party core, the Radicals, studied their plight. Facing party disaster, Lincoln said we had to "play our last card." In January, 1863, they played it: he declared slaves free in all territory not held by his government. He would free the slaves he could not free, and not free the slaves he could. He and even the Abolitionists admitted that the act was illegal; they justified it as a "war measure."

The Emancipation Proclamation had two aims:

1. Incite a slave insurrection;

2. Give their party war a "Cause."

That political act demonstrates Lincoln's indifference to the suffering he hoped to inflict and ignorance of the true black-white relation. His only objection to it, he said, was "that when the Negroes started killing and burning it might play havoc with public opinion in Europe and the North." He spent a fortune on agents and propaganda to incite it, but that part of the Proclamation failed—there was no insurrection. The second aim, fabricating a "Cause," succeeded: the Proclamation did not detach black from white but it did attach "slavery" falsely, to his war. Usurpation found a "Cause." Like the French Revolution the War to Prevent Southern Independence was the city party attacking the agricultural people, the perpetrators fabricating a cause to cover their reach for the Devil's Proposition.

Lincoln's war killed a million people directly; many more from its effects, perhaps a fourth of the black population. He made half of his country a waste land. The *Smithsonian Magazine* reported in 1996 that just a part of his war, Sherman's invasion, was the fourth- severest environmental disaster in North America. Lincoln's destruction was so deep that the South remained poor for a century. White and black suffered and died together. The South, white and colored were a unit. Once they got to eating regular again, the poor South was still a better place to live than the rich North. In unity, harmony, social felicity.

When abolition came it came in the worst possible way, not for the slaves but to serve the interests of the Republican Party in making war. In the South the blacks suffered right along with the whites. In violation of women they suffered more injury by Mrs. Howe's saintly horde than did the whites. Their suffering did not end with the war. Evicted into the cold, their mortality and morbidity remained elevated for decades. Epidemiology estimates that the war killed one-fourth of the Negroes. Mrs. John F. (Julia Hanes) Burnett (Chatham County, N.C.) told her daughter, Florence, that freeing the slaves worked a terrible hardship upon them, that their condition before the war was good and after the war pitiful. One reason was that before "freedom" they were a "family" and able to take care of each other. The war evicted the slaves from that status, to the greater suffering of the Negro.

That such a plight did not befall the Burnett colored people is revealed by this anecdote: As the war ended Mrs. Burnett was sitting discussing the new freedom with Julia, her servant, whose mother, in affection, had named for her mistress. To the younger Burnetts she was "Aunt" Julia. At length, "Miss" Julia asked, "What do you plan to do?" The answer came, "What do I plan? It being bedtime, I plan to go to bed." She went to bed there for the rest of her life. The descendants of both the Julias live yet in the area, still friends and neighbors, though not as intimate as they were before urban employments began to separate people after World War II. Together two hundred-fifty years. The Abolitionists had servants; they were just not as friendly with them.

Lincoln's war injured the slaves during four years of war, then prolonged their suffering four score more years on land he had blighted and the economy he had ruined. The Southern material and physical damage he wrought were slowly repaired decade by decade. His pandemic moral damage will never be. The pernicious result of his forcing the race question into America's public life is irreparable. For selfish power the money party raised the red herring of "slavery," then "race," that equally-false issue, casting that impertinent subject into the political fight between parties. It taught everybody to lie. That dishonest act has done great harm to American society. Its growing evil darkens the unknown future.

Abolition did its greatest harm when the politicians took it up as a red herring to divert attention from their objective—regional abuse. What began as an abstraction, then fantasy, of the leisured, then became an instrument to power. The South seceded to escape injury—financial abuse. They also seceded to escape verbal abuse, and political abuse, and economic abuse using "Abolition" as excuse. Money—taxation—was the cause of secession. "Abolition" was contributory. Abolition frightened the South, it was a sign of enmity. Secession led to war because the ruling party did not want to lose Southern money that would depart with the South. Secession caused the war. Lincoln offered guarantees of slavery, even offered the South every element of freedom except escape of tax. He demanded that the South continue to pay the tariff. Secession was the cause of America's most monstrous crime—Lincoln's war on his own country.

Calling themselves "idealists," Jacobins appeal to man's base nature, their business only a clever scheme of a few to subordinate everybody else. Crying "compassion" they kill people. By methods old as the Bible, Jacobins use slogans, stolen property, and murder to grasp power. The Russian Revolution of 1917 and Chinese Revolution of 1949 were Jacobin enterprises. The War to Prevent Southern Independence in 1861 and the "liberal" movement of 20th century were similar. The Jacobin cries "equality" in order to make himself the elite.

Have you ever known a leftist who was not a gnawing parasite, and an ingrate? It is said that Napoleon first named them Jacobins, mocking the atheists who used Christian shelter to plot its destruction.

A black American has a right to complain. Two revolutions blamed on him; he was innocent of both. The 19th century "slavery issue" was a tool of the money party to take power. Gaining the power, they changed the U.S. Government from a republic to an empire. The second revolution was made possible by the success of the first. The 20th century so-called "Civil Rights

Movement" was the tool of the Communist-Liberal party to take possession of the Democratic Party and thus the U.S. Government. Gaining the government they took away the remaining powers of local governments and private citizens, made the empire all powerful, the citizens all subjects. Both revolutions done in the name of the black people—for the ambition of others. Two revolutions blamed on him. He caused neither. Both did him great injury. The first was physical. The second was physical, mental, and moral. And the second completed the ruin of his country. The United States are now a perfect empire.

Tariff, Tariff, Tariff

"The wealth of the Northern states has been built upon the tribute exacted from the South by the North's dishonest tax policy."

—EDMUND RUFFIN, CREDITED BY THE U.S. DEPARTMENT OF AGRICULTURE WITH MAKING MAJOR CONTRIBUTIONS TO AMERICAN AGRICULTURE

TRADE IS THE MEANS by which people acquire goods and services to sustain life and to enjoy life. Without trade life cannot prosper. After law and order and farming, trade is the next necessity, the lifeblood of all societies above the primitive.

In 1607 the first permanent colony settled in "Virginia." A settlement was called a "plantation," meaning a planting, a permanence, not a temporary visit to trade and leave, but a planting of people and things, to stay. "Plantation" means establishment of a home where there was none. Francis Bacon in 1616 wrote an essay, "Of Plantations." He advised that the planter must, as soon as possible, plant peas and beans, "for they will take the place of meat." Thus the necessity of protein was recognized at least as early as Shakespeare's time.

The South lived on the land and from the land—farm and forest. The Southern planter or farmer lived by trading his products of the land for Europe's products of the hand, manufactures. (Latin: "*manus*" means "hand," "fact" means "do" or "make.") The banks of Southern rivers, from the Delaware to the Sabine, became studded with little docks, loading farm goods destined for Europe and unloading manufactured goods from Europe. The boats were not big, but there were hundreds of them. The Southern farmer could buy the Europeans' manufactures because the Europeans bought his commodities. Little money changed hands; trade between the two really was "trade"—barter—because money was scarce. It was an efficient and balanced exchange.

Exchanging Southern rice, indigo, naval stores, tobacco, grain, foods, timber for European manufactures prospered the Southern colonies. The Southern economy spread westward and was highly productive. Tobacco was the most important American export in the 18th century and cotton made up a large majority of the exports during most of the 19th. The South exceeded the North in population and wealth in 1787 when the Constitution was written. From that moment the decline of the South began due to Northern initiatives in the Federal Congress

Prevailing opinion says that the Southern Independence War was caused by the selfishness of the South and the idealism of the North. After all, were not the Northerners trying to free slaves?

Europeans knew the truth. They have a saying about America: "The North lives for getting and having, the South for being." Never in history has it been said that farmers are more venal than the business class. Even before they left Old England, the Yankees-to-be were already commercial. The future Northerners—Calvinists, Quakers—were already men of town and commerce. The future Southerners were Anglicans or Baptists, farmers. Even then they had a different attitude toward life.

In the New World the divergence widened. The South had little money. But life there was good, the society was kind, the pleasures of company and of nature were easily available, food was so cheap as to be almost free. They needed less money, they were content to have less money, they had no finance industry and they made their money from their own efforts. They did not know much about money. They did not think much about money. "We had everything but money," said Nett Pace (1886-1978). The North had the money.

The money principle divided North and South at the founding. Alexander Hamilton wanted government support for the money men. The money men bought his government paper, thus beginning the mutual benefit of the Federal government and bankers. The Federalist Party of the North advocated a large and powerful central government with broad financial authority, "internal improvements," and tax and tariff policy that benefited capitalists. The agrarian party of the South, Thomas Jefferson's Democratic Republicans, opposed, on principle, such a policy. They declared that government subsidy of private business is immoral, always degenerating into patronage, favoritism, corruption, downright bribery, and inevitably into the tyranny of consolidated power and war. During the 1776 and 1812 wars with England, observers on both sides the ocean said the North was fighting over money, the South for principle.

The Founding Fathers understood that the agricultural South and the mercantile North had conflicting economic interests. They studied the Swiss, who were writing a Constitution themselves, and recognized a common problem. Both nations sought to find the proper form of government for people of diverse interests. Switzerland was one country of two religions, three nationalities, and four languages. The united States were also diverse, widely separated by interests and distance. The countries agreed on the necessary form of government—confederacy. Central governments of people of different interests should be limited, granted only certain specified powers. All other powers should be retained by local governments or by the people privately. Power consolidated is tyranny.

Power diffused—federated—limits tyranny.

The Swiss, wisely jealous of central power, kept power at home, local, never abandoned the principle of federative government, and have prospered in peace, with never a war since. In America, Abraham Lincoln demolished that principle, substituted a centralized rule by party, with the inevitable results of discord, tyranny, waste, patronage, corruption, and war. The consolidation of power that Lincoln made possible controls and blights America today.

Patrick Henry said of the Constitution of 1787, "Those who have no similar interest with the people of the South are to legislate for us. Our dearest rights are to be put in the hands of those whose advantage it will be to infringe them. They will rule by patronage and sword. The states are committing suicide." Charles Cotesworth Pinckney said, "The Southern states are to form a minority, the regulation of trade will be determined by the North. They will profit from our labor." John Tyler Sr. and many others predicted that Northern money interests would become parasites and bring distress on the South.

The new Federal Government established a tariff. The Constitution allowed it to pay the cost of running the central government, which Hamilton's party controlled. It was a disguised tax. The people did not pay it directly, it merely increased the cost of imported goods. It taxed only the South, it subsidized the Northern business class. The South paid that tax as they lived by import-export with Europe, the North did not. The South knew that they were shouldering the burden of the central government, they knew they were subsidizing the North. The South had made most of the sacrifices in the war with Britain: they had furnished the soldiers, they had furnished the money; the battles had been in the South, inflicting injury the North never had. After the war the South had given vast areas of their territory to the North. The South had even shouldered the Northern war debt, having paid their own. The South knew they were sacrificing their welfare in the Constitution. The South submitted. They fondly believed the North would be grateful. It was not to be.

Henry Adams described the Northern parties. Of the politicians who joined Jefferson's party, he said:

> "The new Democrats in New England, New York, and Ohio were Federalists in disguise and cared nothing for the theories of what government might properly do or not do, just so long as the government did what they wanted. They feared no corruption in which they were to have a part. They were in secret jealous of Virginia, and as devoted as George Cabot or Stephen Higginson to the interest of commerce and manufacture. A majority of Northern Democrats were men of this kind. Their dislike of Federalists was a social, not a

political, feeling, for Federalist manners seemed to them a willful impertinence, but the Varnums and Crowninshields of Massachusetts cared as little as De Witt Clinton or Aaron Burr for the small, honest government of Speaker [Nathaniel] Macon and John Randolph. They joined Jefferson's party to profit from his incumbency, and because they were not part of the dominant Federalist Party at home."

That is to say, in the North both parties, for money, would be willing to strangle the South. The world is ruled by interest. The North, already rich, was money-centered. The Northern money party used Congress to enact measures favoring Northern industry at the expense of the South. They raised the tariff: to 20% in 1816, to 37% in 1824, to 50% in 1828. The tariff money the South paid was a subsidy of the Northern economy, transferring money always in the same direction—from South to North. That dominance continued to grow on up to the 1861 war to prevent Southern independence, through the war, and long after the war.

Absence of that tariff protection would have saved the union from war in 1861. Absence of the war would have saved a million lives then and more later. It would have saved their 19th century descendants from the Four Horsemen and their 20th century progeny from the strife of consolidated government, wars, socialism, and race strife.

In 1793 the modern mechanical cotton gin was invented, providing Northern mills a plentiful supply of Southern cotton, the prince of fibers. New Englanders stole from the British the machinery to mass manufacture cloth. The Three-Way Passage gave them riches to invest in factories. That business made the fortunes that made their Abolitionist descendants. There has seldom been so lucrative a trade as the "Three-Way Passage." New England rum went to Africa to buy slaves who went to the West Indies to buy molasses which went to New England to complete a three-way profit. The War of 1812 gave them a new money-making opportunity, manufacturing—supplying war materiel to the government and goods formerly obtained from Europe to the

South. The War of 1812 gave New England manufactures a giant stimulus.

The South looked eagerly to peace. The war had hurt the South: the South had furnished the battlefields, the soldiers, and the money. The South suffered the destruction, the deaths, civilian injury, and economic ruin by the blocking of its trade with Europe. The war had enriched New England. Peace would end their war profits and monopoly of Southern trade. Europe, now back in business, would resume its exchange with the South. New England had grown accustomed to riches. They thought they deserved profits guaranteed by government. They went to Congress and in 1816 won a substantial increase in the tariff. Their tariff increase blocked the South's two-hundred-year trade with Europe. For the next fifty years the Northern-majority Congress raised the tariff on average every five years. They raised it to 20% in 1816, to 37% in 1824, and to 50% in 1828.

John Randolph of Roanoke might be America's most interesting personality, and is surely one of its wisest and noblest characters. Another Southern farmer, perfect aristocrat, he is exceeded by no one in honesty, courage, and devotion to principle. In Congress, 1799-1829, he continually fought to stop the selfish growth of government. He lost that fight, his fellows voted for patronage anyway. But his prediction of the evil result of unchained government has come to pass: loss of freedom, prosperity, security, and peace.

John Randolph called the War of 1812 "the Iliad of our woes." In Congress in 1816 he spoke on the tariff legislation demanded by Northern interests:

> "What you are after is a system of bounties to manufacturers, in order to encourage them to do what, if it is advantageous to do at all, they will do anyway. You are giving a subsidy, a gift, to men to carry out their customary business for their own profit. Your tariff means that government is to give a premium to the manufacturers out of the earnings of the hardworking, hard-pressed farmer. You are injuring our most valuable industry—agriculture. You are about to destroy the industry, agriculture,

that brings to these shores more foreign capital by far than all the manufactures combined.

The question is: Should a farmer be taxed to pay money to a man in Massachusetts who operates a shoe factory or a cotton mill? We can buy cheaper and better products from Europe. It is not fair to lay a duty on the farmer to encourage manufactures. All we shall get from that is worse goods at a higher price. And, the farmer will be paying for everybody's goods. Anybody in the North who buys a pair of shoes will have the Southern farmer subsidizing his purchase.

Why does not the government give a bounty to make flour, or run a grist mill?" We have plenty of them down here in the South. It makes just as much sense. Why should the farmer pay a man more than it is worth to buy clothes made in the North from the farmer's cotton, when, if he can sell his cotton to Europe he can get the money to buy the clothes from Europe? Clothes cheaper and better.

The people of this country have enough burdens without taking on their backs the support of the Northern mill owners. As it is now, five-sixths of the foreign income is brought to this country by the exports of the South. "Two-thirds of the taxes paid in this country are paid by the South. We must not sacrifice one part of our country to enrich the other. What claim does the North have to be supported by the earnings of others? In the late war [of 1812] the farmers bore the whole brunt of the war: paid the taxes that supported it, remained poor, fought in the army. The farmers paid the taxes; the farmers did the fighting. The North started the war because England prohibited their shipping. Then, the war started, the North ran from the fight, threatened to secede, and enriched themselves selling to the army.

The man of commerce is a citizen of no place, or any place. The farmer has his property, his lands, his all, his household gods, to defend, and is like the meek drudge, the ox, who does the labor and plows the ground and then for his reward gets the blighted blades, the moldy straw, and the mildewed shocks of corn for his ration. And the man of commerce, the commercial speculator, lives in riches, and rides in coaches, and rests in palaces. Even without the aid of what Congress gives him, the city money man will beat the farmer every time. Even without Congress's intervention on the other side the farmer is no match for the money man. Alert, vigilant, enterprising and active, the commercial men are collected in masses, come together at a moment's notice to enforce their interest. Do but ring the fire-bell in Philadelphia or Boston, and you can assemble all the town's money men in fifteen minutes. Nay, for that matter, they are already assembled, they are always on Wall Street. Shylock meets his friends there every day. They compare notes, lay plans; they have in trick and intelligence what the farmer can never possess. The ox cannot play the fox or the tiger. A farmer cannot skim into a coffee house and shave a note with one hand, while with the other sign a petition to Congress to relieve him of his burdens by picking the pockets of those whose labors have fed and enriched him, and whose valor has defended him. The farmer, the patient drudges of the other orders of society, will either be left alone, unhurt by taxes and tariff, or forced to pay for the prosperity of the manufacturers, and squeezed by the Northern hand grasping for power."

Thus spoke John Randolph in 1816.

As predicted, the Northern commercial interest used their growing majority in Congress to enact measures increasingly parasitizing Southern agriculture. Abolition was merely the philosophy of a few Northern Jacobin, Humanist zealots, idle intellectuals. The Northern people were indifferent to it. The politicians saw that the Northern wish to keep Negroes out of the North could be used to overcome the opposition. The Northern politicians introduced "slavery" into every subject of dispute with the South in order to distract attention from the real issue—money. It is a perfect illustration of Chancellor Oxenstierne's axiom and lament: "Government is the conduct of public affairs for private interest. It is with so little wisdom that the world is governed." The Abolitionists provided the politicians with a red herring, a vicious and dishonest stratagem that destroyed the body of the South and the soul of the country.

The South was being increasingly separated from its market. Forced away from trade with Europe, the products of which were rendered too costly by the "protective" tariff on imports, the South was forced to buy the more expensive, lower-quality Northern products. The North was selling its manufactured products in a protected and subsidized market; they could set their own prices. The South had to sell in the open, world market. Northern prices rose, Southern prices fell.

The United States were composed of a commercial-manufacturing North and a smaller, weaker, agricultural South. The two regions were split into two parties, representing those antagonistic interests. Five-sixths of the money supporting the central (Federal) government was paid by the South through a tariff. The smaller South paid the tax but the more populous North controlled the Congress and spent the tax to benefit Northern business. The North won twice. The South paid the tariff that prohibited European manufactures from competing with Northern manufactures. The money thus gathered was disbursed by the Northern money men in Northern projects to benefit their business.

In 1824 the Northern majority doubled the tariff: to 37%. Randolph told Congress that the colonies had seceded from England for tax reasons which were a trifle compared to the harm the North was doing the South. He said the South could not stay in the union under such abuse. Nobody, not one person, rose in response to deny the right of a state to leave the union. Twenty-four years later Lincoln affirmed that right. Randolph spoke:

> "If, under the power you have taken to regulate trade, you prevent us from exporting, if you draw the last drop of blood from our veins, the last shilling from our pockets, you have ruined us. What good has the Constitution done us? Its checks and balances have not protected us. A fig for the Constitution. A piece of paper will not protect us from knaves. You ask us to lie down and be shorn. I am surprised that the votaries of humanity—persons who cannot sleep,

so great is their distress of mind at the very existence of Negro slavery—should press so avidly a measure whose effect will be to aggravate the misery of slave and master. What can be more pitiable than a man who has every desire to clothe his Negroes comfortably, but is absolutely prohibited from doing so by Congress? I hope that none of those who wish to raise the price of the slave's (or the master's) blanket or his wool suit, will ever travel through the South and see the nakedness of the land because we cannot export, and the equal nakedness of the cultivators of that land. The profits of slave and master are hardly existent now. The words of Patrick Henry, begging Virginia to remain free outside, not to join the Federal union, ring in my ears: 'They may liberate your slaves. Congress possesses the power, and will exercise it.' Now, the first step toward this event, so devoutly wished by many, is to pass such laws as may yet still further impoverish the masters. You are soon then to see in case the slave will not run away from his master, the master shall run away from him."

John Randolph died in 1833.

Senator Thomas Hart Benton of Missouri said in Congress in 1828:

"I feel for the sad changes in the South. Before the revolution it was the seat of wealth, as well as hospitality. Only the hospitality remains. Wealth has fled the South and settled in the North. The South, in just four of its staples, has since the Revolution, exported eight hundred million dollars, while the North has exported almost nothing. That would indicate wealth unparalleled—but what is the fact? The South is short of money. The frugal habits of the people are pushed to self-denial. Under Federal legislation, the exports of the South have been the basis of the Federal revenue. Virginia, the two Carolinas, and Georgia defray three-fourths of the annual expense of supporting the Federal Government. Of this great sum annually furnished by them, nothing, or next to nothing, is returned to them. That expenditure flows in the opposite direction—it flows northward, in one uniform, uninterrupted, and perennial stream. This is the reason why wealth disappears from the South and rises up in the North. Federal legislation does all this. It does it by eternally taking from the South and returning nothing to it. Every new tariff increases the force of this action. It is Federal legislation that has ruined the South."

In 1828 Congress raised the tariff to 50%. South Carolina threatened to leave the Union. The only issue was the tariff. They were attacked because of money, not slavery. Their opponent was Jackson the slaveholder, not Adams the Abolitionist. It is dishonest to confound the tariff issue with the unrelated subject of slavery.

John C. Calhoun, speaking for South Carolina in 1835, said:

"A deep Constitutional question lies at the bottom of the controversy. The real question is: Has the government a right to impose burdens on the capital and industry of one portion of the country, not with a view to revenue, but to benefit another? The Federal Government has, by express provision of the Constitution, the right to lay duties on imports. The state never denied or resisted this right, nor even thought of so doing. The government has, however, not been contented with exercising this power as she had a right to do, but has gone beyond it, by laying imposts, not for revenue, but for protection. This the state considers as an unconstitutional exercise of power, highly injurious and oppressive to her and the other staple states, and has, accordingly, met it with the most determined resistance. I do not intend to enter, at this time, into the argument as to the unconstitutionality of the protective system. It is not necessary. It is sufficient that the power is nowhere granted; and that, from the journals of the Convention which formed the Constitution, it would seem that it was refused. In a support of the journals, I might cite the statement of Luther Martin, to show that the Convention, so far from conferring the power on the Federal government, left to the states the right to impose duties on imports, with the express view for enabling the several states to protect their own manufactures. Notwithstanding this, Congress has assumed, without any warrant from the Constitution, the right of exercising this most important power, and has so exercised it as to impose a ruinous burden on the labor and capital of the state of South Carolina, by which her resources are exhausted, the enjoyments of her citizens curtailed, the means of education contracted, and all her interests essentially and injuriously affected.

We have been jeeringly told that she is a small state; that her population does not exceed half a million of souls; and that more than one half are not of the European race. The facts are so. I know she never can be a great state, and that the only distinction to which she can aspire must be based on the moral and intellectual acquirements of her sons. To the development of these much of her attention has been directed; but this restrictive system, which has so unjustly exacted the proceeds of her labor, to be bestowed on other sections, has so impaired the resources of the state, that, if not speedily arrested, it will dry up the means of education, and with it deprive her of the only source through which she can aspire to distinction.

The people of the state believe that the Union is a union of states, and not of individuals; that it was formed by the states, and that the citizens of the several states were bound to it through the acts of their several states; that each state ratified the Constitution for itself; and that it was only by such ratification of a state that any obligation was imposed upon the citizens; thus believing, it is the opinion of the people of Carolina that it belongs to the state which has imposed the obligation to declare, in the last resort, the extent of this obligation, so far as her citizens are concerned; and this upon the plain principles which exist in all analogous cases of compact between sovereign bodies. On this principle, the people of the state, acting in their sovereign capacity in convention, precisely as they adopted their own and the federal Constitution, have declared by the ordinance, that the acts of Congress which imposed duties under the authority to lay imports, are acts, not for revenue, as intended by the Constitution, but for their own and the federal Constitution, have declared by the ordinance, that the acts of Congress which imposed duties under the authority to lay imports, are acts, not for revenue, as intended by the Constitution, but for protection, and therefore null and void."

All of the exports, the means of bringing money to our shores, were of the South. The North derived its income from the tariff that forced the South to buy their manufactured goods and from finance and merchant marine that depended on the Southern produce that was exported to the world. The South was indispensable to Northern businessmen. Lincoln was their undeviating agent, always serving their desire for power and profit.

The "revenue" tariff was converted into a "protective" tax on imports to subsidize Northern commerce at the expense of the South. This was what the great economist Ludwig, von Mises called "intervention,"—intrusion by government into what should be private human action. Advanced intervention is called "socialism" or "Communism." "Intervention in the market" mean government invasion of privacy, is always done to benefit one group at the expense of the others, and is always counterproductive. All human action is injured or destroyed when government enters. Most violent wounds, many deaths, and all loss of freedom and prosperity result from the selfish acts of rulers. That is why the South died, it is why the American Republic died. It is the cause of wars. The American tariff story is a classical demonstration that majorities, unless restrained by law, will abuse minorities. Government, unless restrained, will abuse its power.

As we shall see, it was not "the extension of slavery" that moved Lincoln to make war in 1861. It was the loss of profit by wealthy, demanding, and ambitious Northern interests if a vast free trade Confederacy was allowed to flourish in North America.

Talking to Captain Hillyar, of the British Navy, in 1861, the Confederate Navy hero Raphael Semmes said:

> "The North used the machinery of government, in which they had majority power, to enrich the North and despoil the South. They imposed the tariff which reduced the South to a dependent colonial condition like the Roman provinces. The only difference being that the North falsely claimed to be operating under law. Slavery had nothing to do with the war, the hypocritical Yankees care nothing for the Negroes. The slavery issue is only a by-play, a device to cover Northern grasp for empire—power. The North only began the slavery agitation when they began to rob the South by raising the tariff. The slavery issue was only a diversion, it was no more than an implement used by a robber to rob the South. Finally, realizing the North would never treat us fairly, the South withdrew from the union. We merely want to be independent. We are fighting for our independence because the North does not want to lose their milk cow and has attacked us, to forcibly hold us to pay their bills."

Many Americans saw the tariff's selfish motive, and foresaw its harmful effects and evil results. The position of the South on the tariff is today, two hundred years later, held by lovers of freedom to be economically and morally correct. Can you improve this truth?

Can you gild the lily?

Territorial Expansion

"Politics – A strife of interest pretending to be a contest of principle."

—AMBROSE BIERCE

"The whole aim of practical politics is to keep the populace alarmed, to produce in their minds fear, so that they will be willing to be led to 'safety.'"

—H.L. MENCKEN

LONG BEFORE AMERICANS CEASED FIGHTING foreigners and Indians for possession of territory they began fighting each other for it. Man is a territorial animal, he cannot see principles but he can feel space. There is no area of life that the politician, that most selfish of animals, will not intrude into, distort shamelessly, if he can use it. None too remote, none too unrelated. Unless he is chained he will stop at nothing. Government officers must be chained.

The selfish character of the politician is perfectly demonstrated by America's accession of new land. No subject would seem to be less attractive to a politician than land. What could be more unrelated to politics than the farmers' need for land? No politician is going to farm it. The farmers had a simple, honest desire to get a farm, cultivate it, and raise a crop. The politicians cultivated that need to their use, to raise an "issue." They brought a simple need to a horrible result.

Thirteen separate colonies seceded from Britain and formed thirteen separate states. The colonies had conflict between Southern farmer and Northern finance from the beginning. When they became states the fight turned mean.

Virginia, with her own money and blood, won the war with Britain for possession of the Northwest Territory. The Northern states had no investment in it and never paid their debt to the South. Virginia, in noblesse, gave the Northwest Territory to all the states. Then Virginia, in good will, ceded part of its territory across the mountains, Kentucky, so it could govern itself. North Carolina and Georgia did the same with their western lands.

The statehood quarrel was simply a matter of party rivalry—money and power.

Would the new states join Jefferson's small-government party or the big-government party of Adams and Hamilton? The farmer party wanted a central government of limited powers, not able to spend tax money patronizing favorites. The merchant party wanted just the opposite—a government to subsidize their business.

First: tariff, then territory. The money party flung the unrelated subject of "slavery" into the transaction of admitting the new state of Missouri (1819). Most of the migrants to Missouri were Southern farmers. Farmers had been planting themselves into Missouri's rich lands for some years. In 1818 Missouri Territory applied to join the union. The Northern Federalist Party, to block Jeffersonian Americans from gaining another state, denied the right of slaveholders to move there. Some were already there. It was clearly unfair to deny Southern right to use the territories. The South had signed the Constitution with no apprehension that their rights in the territories were to be abridged. They had to pay the taxes the North escaped. Now they were to be excluded from new territory that the North could freely enter.

The money party first declared they would not vote Missouri into the union unless slavery was excluded. That rule would deny some Southern farmers the right to settle there and invalidate the constitution recently created by the people of Missouri. John

Randolph of Roanoke begged Congress not to surrender the Constitutional prohibition against federal interference in the internal affairs of a sovereign people. But some Southerners in a spirit of peace accepted the Missouri Compromise. In this so-called "compromise" Southerners were allowed into Missouri but would be excluded from most of the remaining lands of the Louisiana Purchase.

The Missouri Compromise changed the rules. It redefined the Constitution. The great principle that protected the states was surrendered. John Randolph said if principle had been maintained, the politicians could never more have raised that false issue, "slavery," to confound the regional money quarrel. All the later horrors would have been prevented. The millions murdered would have lived. Allowing the Federal Government to enter the internal affairs of a state has let it cannibalize all the states. The Missouri Compromise was no compromise, it was a defeat for the South, and for the whole country. It allowed the Federal Government to define its own powers, to replace republic by empire, to destroy freedom. The Missouri Compromise was fatal. Randolph did not live to see the horrible fulfillment of his prophecy.

Moral opposition to "slavery" hereafter would be the money party's excuse. Thomas Jefferson and James Madison said the Northern attack was not sincere and benevolent but an immoral tactic to divorce the agricultural West from the agricultural South and rescue the discredited Federalist Party. The Constitution prohibited Federal Government intrusion in slavery. The South should have seceded right then.

The argument over territories, to become new states, related to the tariff. If settled by Southerners they would vote against the tariff and against the Northern program. The North opposed new territories and states, they did not need new land and they believed that new states would send delegations to Congress that would vote against the subsidy policy. The tariff was the most important element of the subsidy but there were many others. Northern opposition to new territory and new states further injured the South.

The money party proved to be just as dishonest and hateful in fighting acquisition of every territory and admission of any state expected to join the farmer party. In 1804 New England, opposing Louisiana, threatened to secede.

A Kentuckian named Levi Todd called the interference with Missouri "dishonest and hateful." He would have a granddaughter named Mary. Her husband would be a fixed agent of the Northern money party, would make war on the farmer party. He would hide his private ambition under a dishonest public opposition to slavery. To acquire power he would make a hateful political war on the Todds and countless others like them. To keep power, he would make a more a savage armed war on the Todds—and kill some of them.

The year 1820 was a bad one for the United States—their Constitution was dealt a blow from which it has never recovered. The peoples of the states had made a confederacy, a federal system of government, the structure to protect freedom by retaining local power, by limiting the power given the central government. Government by the people is local government, enforced by retained power, maintained by a system of state's rights. That is the universal necessity of freedom. Tyranny is the natural result of consolidated power.

Territory meant Congressional seats—would they be farm or finance? The Northern money party wanted to elect a Federal Government that would subsidize their business. A party cannot win elections on such a platform. They could not make attractive their demands for government favor.

The money party used "slavery" to cover an unrelated regional power quarrel, first their abuse of government for money, then their abuse of new state admissions, and then to cover their chase for executive power. Ever since Thomas Jefferson was elected in 1800 the money party had gained increasing majority in Congress. But, in all that time, every four years something happened to deny them the presidency. True, they had elected John Quincy Adams in 1824, but the rising power of Andrew Jackson weakened, then canceled, it. Even the two Whigs they elected (1840, 1848) would not satisfy their demands. The money party was angry and mean. They were vicious to the unyielding presidents, Tyler and Polk. For money.

Not slavery.

For a while, the "slavery issue" petered out. "Slavery" was quiet. The politicians had no use in it. People on the Southern farms were left alone. The South did not have money, but they had a happy life. The life of a slave could not have been too onerous. 19th century mariners visiting Haiti observed that there were more women than men, learned that the men, for the good life, shipped out to the Southern United States for work.

The money party politicians were not happy in the 1840s. They had lost office, but not ambition. Out of power a long time, they were frustrated. Their party—called successively, Federalist, anti-Jackson, Whig, anti-Democrat, anti-Douglas, Republican—was the party of commerce. An Illinois politician, Abraham Lincoln, was an undeviating agent of that faction, promoting tariff increases, "internal improvements," national bank, and business subsidy—all paid by the South. That was a hard platform to run on. Who would vote for a platform to enrich the rich? The Democrats were steadily outdistancing them.

The ordinary citizen is unaware of the struggle for government office, the real motive of his public officers, the lust for the power of rule. The individual voter is not the party, he is only the dupe who in numbers makes possible the party. The party is the inside elite, who control and profit by it. The individual thinks his political leaders are fighting for principle. They are not fighting for principle, they are fighting for place—the kingdom and the power and the glory of office. And for the profit of those interests which help them obtain place. They don't care about the citizens, their subjects, they want to surmount them, gain a place higher than their fellows. For power they will, if necessary, kill them.

In 1847 the "Chicago Rivers and Harbors Convention," a group of Northern politicians and businessmen, met to form a lobby to extract money from Congress. It was in essence a Northern Whig convention. The Southern Whigs, able to see the corruption in "internal improvements," did not attend. Abraham Lincoln saw fit to attend. He wanted them to know their man. He knew that group was his river to Snug Harbor. Those men were the backbone of the Federalist-Whig-Republicans. Their real interest was money but "slavery" would hide it. Their enemy was Southern Democrats in Congress voting against their profitable subsidies. They opposed President Polk's frugal government. They opposed admitting to the union any new states expected to vote Democratic.

Money, not slavery, was the party's subject and object. Later, Lincoln tried to blame his war on the black man. The black man had nothing to do with it. He was only an excuse to cover the real reason—money. What the powerful men at that convention did mention was money, patronage, and power. They were angry at Southerners for blocking government policies subsidizing their profits. These were the men who would make war for money.

Slave-trading profits created what was called an aristocracy in New England, that money-based society. Slavery had been found to be of little economic value in the North. The North had ended slavery by gradual selling slaves South and subsidized programs of emancipation. They took no monetary loss. The South had freed far more black people, that is, gave them freedom while the North sold or abandoned theirs. Who was saint and who was sinner? Slavery in the North still had not completely ended when its politicians dishonestly made the "slavery issue" central to territorial expansion.

Enter the Politician

"The national conflict was not between the Southern people and Northern people, it was between the Southern people and the Northern politicians."

—DANIEL HACKNEY

"No man who is a lover of glory can be said to be a lover of his fellow men."

—EPICTETUS, 60:120

"The agitation of the slavery issue is nothing more than the unprincipled conduct of ambitious men."

—JOHN RANDOLPH OF ROANOKE

Definition: AMBITION. From Latin "AMBITIO," "a going around for votes, self-promotion; an eager or inordinate desire for preferment, superiority, or power."

"POLITICIAN" COMES FROM THE GREEK word, "polis," for "city," the government unit of ancient time. "Police" means "city officer." "Politician" meant one who conducts "city" [government] affairs. Now it means a government-job hunter.

Groups must have government. Governments must have officers to conduct their business. There is the rub. The citizen thinks that the interests of the people and the interests of the politicians are the same. They are not the same. The ordinary citizen does not know how rich are the rewards of office nor how far men will go to get them. Politicians are interested in self, not in others, in principal, not principle. Officers like office more than they like people. They are in office because they like power. Given power they will take more, if they can. The only interest of a political party is power. The people want peace, to be let alone. The politicians want power, will disturb the people, use any weapon, including war, to get it. That is why government power must be limited, government officers chained. Ambition—worldly power—the Devil's Proposition.

Lincoln's ambition never rested. Perceiving that trait did not wait the mature reflection of history, it was marked in his youth. Before he was twenty-one he said he was going to be president of the United States. He spent the rest of his life on that track, and he had a one-track mind. His lawyer peers said he was the most single-minded political figure in America, "America's most adroit politician."

William Herndon, as assiduous as Boswell, gathered information on Lincoln: Lincoln's closest acquaintances said he had no philosophy, no principle, and no religion. He was directed by policy, his policy directed by party, by what was expedient to his advance. He was a man of the time and the place, choosing his words to fit the moment and the audience, using public events and popular movements to promote his career, never risking a stand that might cost him votes. Outside politics he knew nothing. He did sip some of the Humanist cup, that will corrupt fools always, even angels sometimes. A little knowledge is a dangerous thing. Deadly when drunk from a party spring. "He never read a book through. If a book came into his hands he might turn the pages for phrases to ornament his speeches." "He had no knowledge, no business, no judgment." To popularize himself he became a traveling lecturer. So defective was his understanding that his friends were embarrassed for him, ordered him to quit, to never talk on any subject but politics. He courted the Abolitionists, hiding it as he hid his atheism. When it suited his use "he became our abolitionist agent." Policy, not principle.

William Seward knew two men well. He said Jefferson Davis never told a lie and Lincoln never told the truth. Of Davis: "His private and public thoughts were the same." Of Lincoln: "All his words were to a purpose." "He had a cunning that was genius." Charles Francis Adams was shocked at Lincoln's crude and cynical nature.

The man who put on the humble mask in politics, who called himself "humble," his peers called self-important, self-confident, self-absorbed, "thinks he can do anything," "regards himself superior to everybody." There was no more assertive or self-promoting member of the Illinois Legislature. Where was his humility, this lawyer who collected a $5,000 fee, married into one of the most prominent families in the west, his wife a social leader, he one who took charge of every group? He worked to be the center of every gathering, entertaining, performing, but never candid. He sought popularity without friendship, familiarity without intimacy. His closest associates said they never knew him. Herndon said Lincoln's peers, those who knew him best, did not like him, that his popularity was with the distant public, Lincoln's "common man."

A lifelong agent of the money party, he was reckless with public money. He aggressively led the legislature to spending the Illinois government into insolvency. Close with his own money; he was free with the money of others. He parasitized personal acquaintances, let them support him, after using them left them without gratitude. He let debts run for years. "He did no charity—individual or institutional." "He had not avarice, but had no generosity." "He had not the sin of the 'git', but he lacked the goodness of the 'give'," said Herndon. Indifferent to business, he evaded administration and management, made others attend his personal business, was fortunate to have associates to do it for him. He was a hard worker in politics but confined his work to vote-getting. He never would preside over even a political meeting. Zealous in campaign, he evaded work when elected. As candidate he wrote thousands of letters; as president "he wrote and read less than one letter a day. We read, and wrote them," said Nicolay and Hay.

In 1847, after six years of striving, he at last elbowed his way into the United States Congress. He was a Whig, but the president was a Democrat. James Knox Polk ranks among the best of American presidents in integrity and accomplishment. It is not his substantial achievements that attracts history's attention, but the party strife, the turmoil stirred by the resentful money party. Money and power, disguised as anti-slavery. The money party, then called "Whig," attacked Polk as they had Tyler for resisting their abuse of government for private interest. The frustrated Whigs sought some way to split Northern and Southern Democrats.

Gaining Congress did not gain Lincoln satisfaction. Congress was a mere way-station, necessary to further climbing. He was never satisfied, never modest, however skillfully he played the role. He wanted to look humble in order not to be humble. He wanted "the common people," as he called them, to lift him above them. He wanted to rise. But first he needed to be noticed. To be noticed he needed a subject.

The only subject of national interest was the Mexican War. As a candidate Lincoln had favored the war which the Illinois electorate strongly supported. The Northern money men did not want Texas or any other new states. After fifty years of failing to block acquisition of new territory, their hostility to new states had grown fierce. The South-hating ex-President John Quincy Adams, now in the House of Representatives, fulminated against Texas. Reminded that in 1819 he had claimed Texas down to the Rio Grande as possessed by the United States he did not cease his abuse.

Working to exclude Texas and any new states that would join the farm party, the Whigs pushed the Wilmot Proviso, a measure to exclude slavery from all new territory derived from the war. Congressman David Wilmot, a pro-tariff Democrat from Pennsylvania, said its purpose was to reserve all new lands for

"White Men." Lincoln said he voted for the Wilmot Proviso "forty times." Looking to rise in the party, Lincoln courted the Eastern Whigs. Ambition overcame prudence. His first month in Congress he joined their aggressive attack on President Polk, Texas, and the Mexican War. He developed a speech asking for the "Spot" where something happened that required war. Polk ignored Lincoln. Lincoln acquired ridicule and the name "Spotty."

During his one-term Congressional career he took two significant positions:

1. The president has no constitutional power to start a war.

2. Any people have the right to seek self-government.

Thirteen years later: (1) he started a war (2) to prevent secession. The only purpose of his war was to prevent secession. In the most fateful attack on freedom of any American president, he denied the two fundamental principles of freedom: limited government power and right to withdraw.

President Polk took no notice of Lincoln's attack. The Western Whigs did. To his dismay they refused to re-nominate him. Lincoln's conduct had so discredited the party that in the safest Whig district in Illinois, Lincoln's successor nominee was defeated.

Knocked off the stairs to power, the power-seeker fell into deep depression. Having to pack up and leave Washington, D.C., devastated him. Slow to vacate, he spent a year soliciting a government job—writing letters, talking to politicians, traveling. He complained to President Zachary Taylor that nobody more deserved a job, that nobody was a better party man than he. He was right, there was never a better party hack than Abraham Lincoln. He had worked hard for Taylor. The man who could not bear the thought of slavery never gave it a thought that Taylor was a slaveholder. He had campaigned three times for slaveholder Henry Clay. He traveled to Lexington, Kentucky, to enter a lawsuit for possession of Todd family slaves. He took his money in transactions concerning slaves.

President Taylor did offer Lincoln a minor job. Lincoln decided it held little prospect for advancement, so he declined it. After a year's seeking, he had to admit defeat, return to his boring law practice, to the District that had spurned him and would vote against him again. He had lost everything that meant anything, after trying harder than anybody.

In 1849, forced out of Congress by his attention-seeking attack on President Polk, unable to get a government job, Abraham Lincoln had no choice but to return to work. He never liked law, or any work, stayed out of the office when he could, had no interests but politics; was most interested in self-promotion and worked ceaselessly to raise himself in the party. He was frustrated and depressed because he had no way to raise himself before the public. He needed an issue. To a politician an "issue" is only a vehicle, a necessary carriage to comfort.

The "slavery issue" went dormant for a while. The Whig Abraham Lincoln appealed for votes by accusing Democrat opponents Franklin Pierce and Martin Van Buren of being against slavery. He campaigned in 1852 against the "vile agitation of the slavery issue." The man history calls the moral hater of slavery found no objection to it when it when his own candidates were slaveholders. Two years later he labeled slavery a crime, one section of the country saints, the other, sinners. "Slavery" did not call his attention until he saw it could call attention to him.

He dragged himself back to the law office of "Lincoln and Herndon." Herndon had been operating the office for three years. Lincoln let him do it awhile longer. Refusing to work, he lay listless on the sofa, brooding on his wrongs. Experience is the only teacher, bitter experience the best. Lincoln had wanted the Eastern Whigs to notice him. The western Whigs noticed, and rejected him. But he learned. To start a war you must have or make a "reason," a "spot," or a "shot." Once started, it has momentum of its own, it is a hard engine to stop. He could not recruit opposition to the Mexican War—patriotism is a strong emotion. Aiming to wound the Democrats, he had shot himself. His attempt to make an issue had ruined him. But he had his lesson; he thought long on it. Next time he would know how to use it. His pride wound gave him instruction that he would use to inflict a mortal wound on his country.

At last he went back to work. But not in the office. Requiring the submissive Herndon to continue office confinement, Lincoln stayed out on the court circuit, free of chores and free to politic. He made himself a traveling entertainer, known in every crossroads tavern. He cultivated lawyers, local leaders, and politicians, made contacts, built connections. He used his ample leisure to write self-promoting letters by the hundreds. He shook hands with everybody, made personal acquaintance with more people in the district than any other man. The near public knew him, the Whig politicians even outside Illinois knew him, but the distant public did not know him. He was the busiest Whig in party affairs, but he had no way to spread his name.

In 1854-1855 he tried for election to the Senate. In that election there was no use for "slavery" agitation, so he did not agitate it. He was not running against the Democratic Party, he was running as an individual politician against other individual politicians. It was the state legislators whose vote he wanted. The politicians chose another ambitious politician. Lincoln resented Lyman Trumbull but was too clever to show it. He would need and use him and his supporters later.

Lincoln Gets Off the Couch

"The very essence of a free government consists in considering offices as public trusts, bestowed for the good of the country, not for the benefit of an individual or a party.

That system of political morals which regards offices in a different light, as public prizes to be won by combatants most skilled in the arts and corruption of political tactics, to be used and enjoyed as their proper spoils—strikes a fatal blow at the very vitals of free institutions"

—JOHN C. CALHOUN

IN 1848 THE WHIG PARTY began dissolving. Regarded as a club seeking favor for the wealthy, for forty years they had used their growing Congressional majority to favor themselves at the expense of the Southern exporting-farmer. The farmers complained, without relief. The money party's politicians increased the abuse. They were living in ease off Southern money. But they, too, were unhappy. They did not have it all—they lacked the presidency. "Slavery" was a contrived issue, but they had no other. The money men assumed a "moral" stand.

In 1854 the Whig name expired, went the way of the Federalists.

That orphaned the money party politicians. A politician without a party has no vehicle, no chance for office. These men, these non-Democrats, were lost in limbo. They had to have some reason for being. "Slavery" was all they had. But nobody listened.

The Northern remnants of the Whig Party had two desires: prevent the admission of new states expected to be Democrat and find some way to weaken the powerful Democrat Stephen A. Douglas, widely expected to be the future president. Douglas had the incumbency and the ascendancy in Illinois, and great national standing. The non-Democrats in the North were out of office and out of power.

Douglas inadvertently breathed life into the languishing body. Happenstance, political chance, smiled on Abraham Lincoln more than any other American politician. External events rescued him from obscurity. In 1854 Senator Douglas, as chairman of the Committee on Territories, was required to fashion a bill to convert the Kansas-Nebraska territory into states. Douglas wrote a bill which he considered a mere mechanism. It used "popular sovereignty," by which inhabitants of the territory would decide local issues, including slavery.

So, the non-Democrats took up the Abolitionists' false issue and accused the Democrats of abetting the spread of slavery to the North. They made great noise about Douglas repealing the Missouri Compromise, although they had not supported it and had tried themselves to revoke it. "This slavery thing" would give Lincoln an issue, a chance to campaign, something to say to serve and mask ambition. Up to now, languishing in his law office, he could not just get up from his sofa where he lay, nursing his dreams of power, and go out and campaign for office. He had tried it and failed. Who would listen? What could he say? Where would he get an audience?

Senator Douglas's bill provided that the settlers of the two new territories, Kansas and Nebraska, could vote on whether to allow Missouri farmers to bring in their servants. The matter should have been let alone, slavery would have amounted to nothing there, would have gradually petered out. But the Abolitionists and politicians raised the "anti-slavery" cry, that it was immoral to allow "the expansion of slavery." (Jefferson had pointed out long ago that slaves moving from one place to another did not expand the number of slaves.) Lincoln ran to it. His political associates said he used public sentiment, popular movements to advance himself. He tested the wind of public opinion, then ran to get in the front of it.

Douglas had provided the "anti-Democrat" politicians (they did not yet have a name) an issue. A perfect red herring for Lincoln. "He became our abolitionist leader," wrote Herndon. The commerce party used the technique of stigmatizing the South as "the slave power" to distract attention from the real questions, to confuse all subjects so as to cover their self-serving. "Anti-slavery" was really "anti-Negro." The western states had voted to exclude them from residence and citizenship.

It all had to do with power and money. Where was the moral? What was moral about "The Secret Six," the wealthy New Englanders who sponsored the opportunist-sociopath, demented John Brown to go to Kansas to kill, to try to make a sectional war?

Kansas-Nebraska was a perfect issue, applying only to the opposite party. Lincoln counted up the benefits. The Northern money party had long ago sold off their slaves. They could label the Democrats as evil. The ordinary citizen up North did not want the black people migrating into their states. The Northern legislatures, Lincoln's included, had voted exclusion. A further benefit was that the Northern money men would welcome any means of getting the greed party into the White House. They wanted a National Bank, internal improvements, and tariff. The agricultural Democrats needed new land to farm. The Northern money men opposed new territory. They made their money at home, in the Eastern counting-houses.

The people who wanted to live in Kansas were Southern farmers by way of Missouri. Some were already there. A few owned slaves. There were few slaves in Kansas, none in Nebraska. Slavery would never amount to anything in either state but the money men did not want the South to have Kansas. The legitimate settlers there were Southern. In those days, before Edmund Ruffin found the cause and the cure, lands "wore out" while the world demand for Southern products continued to grow. At first there were so few Northerners settling in Kansas that the money party had to recruit mercenaries to go there to start a war. The Southern position was that they had signed the Constitution with no suggestion that they would lose their right to move into new territory. The Constitution prohibited Federal Government intrusion into local affairs, specifically slavery.

If the farmers had been allowed to move into Kansas it would have done no harm. It was not even certain the state would become Democrat; the West, too, was developing an appetite for government money. The party could let the states come in, let the country rest, spare the people. But Kansas gave the money party a chance to use "slavery" against the opponents of their agenda, a chance too promising to lose. The party could confound Kansas admission with "slavery," confuse the national mind with tumult, injure Douglas and the Democrats in both sections. The choice was theirs.

They did what politicians always do, chose their interest, not the people's. The "public servants" served themselves at the expense of the public. False as it was, they went to the fish box, grabbed the stinking red herring they had selfishly used to vex the country for forty years. They threw "slavery" onto an unrelated business, a routine transaction. Kansas-Nebraska was a perfect opportunity for the money party to use the red herring. There was no risk in it for them. It would lose few votes in the North. The North was remote from slavery, ignorant of it and of black people. Slavery was distant, an abstraction. "Anti-slavery" could be presented as appealingly "moral."

The party cared nothing for the slaves: Abolitionists said so. But they loved "slavery." The politicians, not the people, forced "slavery" on the nation. Why Lincoln did it is clearly described by Herndon: "Lincoln knew he was politically dead. He despaired of ever rising again. He was sad, unsocial, abstracted. In the Kansas-Nebraska Bill he saw his opportunity and Douglas's downfall. He instantly entered the political field. From 1854 to 1861 he was in his glory, "had high hopes to fill his aspirations," according to Herndon. Herndon was with Lincoln when he heard the news and reports that Lincoln was excited, rejuvenated, saw a way to get back into public notice.

The aim of practical politics is to alarm the populace, to produce fear in their minds so that they will be willing to be led to "safety." The voters had ignored "slavery" after the issues raised by the Wilmot Proviso had been settled by "the Compromise of 1850." The money party saw a way to force it on their attention: Define the "issue" not as a principle but as a personal threat, the "peril" of Negro invasion. It was dishonest. The Negro was no menace to the West. The "issue" was a lie.

But the "issue" of slavery was a perfect red herring for the Northern money party. It gave the politicians an excuse to run, something to say. Without "slavery" Lincoln could not have gotten off his couch. What could he say? "Vote for me so I can get out of this boring law office and savor the power I crave?" "Slavery" would attract attention to the politician.

"Slavery" was the best red herring in the history of politics. It seemed so virtuous, appealing to the abstract philanthropy in everybody. It was exciting, putting emotion in place of practical thought. Attracting attention, it distracted attention from the real issue, a party putting their interest above the nation's interest. What was better for the people—Douglas's quiet or Lincoln's strife; Douglas's peace or Lincoln's war?

In a democratic form of government election is conferred by the broad mass of population—strangers. Some means must be found to attract their notice, and then offer them something. Issues, therefore, are sought — magnified, or manufactured. The aspirant promotes himself by agitating. "Demagogue" means "people stirrer." That is the great weakness of a democracy compared to a republic.

In a republic, a representative system, local officers are elected by local people who know them. Those officers, or representatives, go on to elect others whom they know, so that all officers are elected by people who know them personally.

A democracy must appeal to the lowest denominator and farthest stranger. To excite the farthest stranger requires an extreme issue. That requires demagoguery, stirring and heating the mass in order to rise from the mass. The politician does not rise by favor conferred by acquaintances, his peers who personally know him as a man of probity. It is strangers he must attract, he must be a public showman. That is why politicians are always crying, "I view with alarm," seeking to agitate rather than to assuage public order. That is why "issues" are sought, raised, and even made law. That is why political philosophers say that all government action is done for the politicians, not the people, and is destructive. Lincoln won office by fabricating a nonexistent peril.

The money party did not care about slaves, free Negroes, or whites. Or the country. They cared about place, plunder, and power. They wanted Douglas's place and his party's power. Blaming the Democrats for "spreading slavery" was dishonest and untrue, but it would injure them. The "unprincipled conduct of ambitious men" raised a hue and cry along the line that the Abolitionists had influenced, from New England, through Northern New York, into Ohio, Michigan, Northern Indiana, Northern Illinois, and Iowa. The party alarmed the North.

Lincoln favored the Illinois Negro-exclusion laws. Forgotten today, that attitude was the basis of the Northern and Western opposition to "slavery moving north." Lincoln threatened the gullible European immigrants through newspapers that he secretly owned with the lie that Negroes would spread to their neighborhoods and that the South intended to enslave the immigrants. He deliberately sold a false scenario to set the Northern public against the South. The war the Republican Party engendered and Lincoln made was not a false threat, it was a real disaster.

Lincoln wanted place. He had served his party, slaveholder and non-slaveholder alike. His career "was not service to any principle, but pursuit of office, using popular movements to gain attention." The politicians started barking "slavery" and never stopped until they had unleashed the dogs of war. They made "slavery" take possession of public life, excluding real national needs. Their false fire consumed the Union.

Outside the party councils Lincoln was stirring. The morality of slavery was his vehicle for agitation propaganda. His speeches were not factual, none addressed the practical treatment of the institution. Douglas, naively, was specific, candid, practical. Lincoln said slavery was a great peril. To Lincoln all was political. He was not interested in settling any question, just settling himself in Washington. His words were cant—vague, safe, fashioned to that goal. His faction, the Whig orphans, took up "slavery" to take power. Meeting first as "anti-Douglas," they had to have a name. They eventually chose the name "Republican" to draw on the popularity of Thomas Jefferson's old Republicans, a party of totally opposite principle.

They made an "issue" of an institution unrelated to the regional quarrel. But it was a perfect red herring for the money party. It was regional, so agitating about it would not bother their constituents. It was removed at distance, few in the North knew what it really was, it could be distorted easily for party use. "Anti-slavery" appealed to the abstract philanthropy in all humans, even hypocrites and criminals. And, as a free gift, the Abolitionists would do their work for them. "Slavery" was not the question, it was intruded to divert attention from the real dispute, their greed. It was a tool.

This new club, this new party, a faction whose common interest was to take the offices of the Democrats and use "slavery" to cover it, gathered together in Bloomington, Illinois, in 1856. They called themselves "Delegates." Who had delegated them? Nobody. They had delegated themselves. What were they? They were non-Democrats, envious of Democrat incumbency. These anti-Douglas, anti-Democrat politicians were a group, but they did not have a constituency. To be a party they had to have a constituency. To get voters they had to find some issue to attract them, to excite them. Better, to frighten them.

So, they threw in the red herring. They pictured "slavery" as a danger. The party needed a speaker skilled in cant and in agitation, who could dissemble enough to give them the proper slogans. They picked Lincoln. He was a haranguer, he reduced every subject to slogan. He was the best at using words to stir without telling the truth. Lincoln, always a "trimmer," had not yet joined their pack, but he would be their barker. They would bark "slavery" and never stop until they had won power.

Lincoln was the best agitator, agitation his practice. He spent weeks preparing his speech for the new party. He knew that a successful performance would lift him to the front. They wanted a violent attack on the Democrats as the party of slavery. They wanted to formulate words that would draw attention. No reporters were allowed in the room. The doors were locked. Lincoln did not disappoint his fellows. He gave them what they wanted, the way to use the slaves to serve the party. He said the nation was in great danger. The South would spread slavery over the nation, the South was evil, his party the moral people who would put slavery on the way to extinction. What would happen to the South and its black people was not addressed. His immediate enemy was not the South but the Northern Democrats.

He did not let his words get outside the room but showed the politicians how to fabricate an "issue" and make a campaign theme. What he was after was to be the standard bearer for the party that was going to mount the "slavery issue" and ride it roughshod to plunder. They were not after helping the nation, just themselves.

They would light a fire. They would burn the nation to possess it. Violent, hostile talk would attract the party to him but repel many voters. He would not let his speech be read, printed or out of his hands. It did its work. From that moment (June 1856), with that one issue, his associates said, "Lincoln was a full-time candidate for the presidency."

The man picked to speak to the party would be the last to join the party. He did not know if it would prosper. The "trimmer" waited to be sure how the wind was blowing. If the party sank he did not want to go down with it. His fellow politicians said he never took a stand against public opinion. When he was sure the new party would be the Whig successor and when the party began to lose patience with him, he joined it.

Lincoln and Herndon, by broadsheet and newspaper, invited the public to the important meeting to establish a Springfield chapter of the Republican Party. "The nation is in peril, there is a national need, and public demand for the new party to solve the nation's problems." So said their advertisements. The public was not so alarmed, there were only three people at the meeting—Lincoln, Herndon, and an idle man who happened to be at the court house. His name was put on a public statement as a member of the "committee." Lincoln was disappointed, but worried none over it; he knew how politics worked. He and Herndon controlled the local Whig paper, wrote its editorials, wrote its "news" when they desired. He wrote a report of the meeting as though it was widely attended. He knew what to do. He now had what he needed: an "issue" and a party, something to sell, and a vehicle to carry it—Snake Root and Buggy.

From 1856 the indolent lawyer whose "ambition never rested" lived the life he loved. He had excuse to flee the office, freedom to pursue his lust. The "full-time candidate for president" traveled over Illinois and contiguous states, wrote letters by the thousands. Nicolay and Hay said in campaign zeal he was chief but that once in office he did little work. "We did most of it. He wrote less than one letter a day, read hardly more. We read and wrote almost all his correspondence. Most of it he did not even read."

For five years the indolent man was stimulated, the showman was in his element. The mountebank could play the role of missionary to court his god, Power. He could wear the costume of crusader seeking to destroy vice while pursuing the cardinal one. How idealistic, how safely in fashion! The Abolitionists would do his work for him, even make him seem a moderate. What a patriot! What a statesman! What a role! Not a single lawyer or politician ever called him a missionary. His cronies said the presidency was Lincoln's goal but he would never permit a hint at it. The actor played his "modesty" part, the public servant, willing to serve the ideal. He cared nothing for the slave or for anyone else. His interest was himself. His partner, Herndon, stayed in the law office.

Lincoln demonstrated that his interest was career, not country. He told his party to keep the attention of the people on "slavery," do not let their attention be diverted to other issues. He told them that if the Democrats introduced another subject to ignore it, go back to slavery. If there was ever a proof that politics is a strife of interest pretending to be a contest of principle, the power struggle of 1854-1860 is it.

He won the Republican nomination to run against Douglas for the Senate. He asked Douglas to enter a series of debates at different towns about Illinois. Douglas should never have consented to give publicity to an unknown. But Douglas never ran from a fight. The debates released Lincoln from the closet and bound Douglas in the coils of the "slavery issue." Lincoln would talk of nothing but "slavery." He talked it one way to the old Americans in southern Illinois and quite another to the recent immigrants and New Englanders in the north. He was a one-issue candidate, and that one false. Lincoln was vague, mystical, anecdotal, moral, and impossible to pin down. "Slavery" was the classical red herring but it did its work.

It got the actor a starring role.

The 1858 Illinois Senate race was the first round in the fight for the presidency.

The presidency was Lincoln's real aim. Douglas defeated Lincoln for the Senate in 1858, but at the cost of the presidency. Lincoln made a show, a circus, of a serious subject. His distortions were more effective than Douglas's truths. Many voters were taken in by the confidence man. It is vain to try to dignify what he did. The result of the campaign for power that he conducted from 1854 to 1860 was injury to the people and government, but he has never been indicted for it. Such is the power of power. Victory, success, is worshiped, no matter how destructive.

Abraham Lincoln was a classical party politician," never deviating from the money party's program of rewarding itself with Federal money. Money mostly taken from the South. As candidate he promised, as president he executed, the highest tariff in history. In politics the money man pretended to be the poor boy, affecting simplicity and humility; in private life he showed the egotistic superiority he really felt. Lincoln and party would execute the policy of the Eastern industrialists and bankers—tax the South to pay themselves. That policy had limited appeal, even in the North. The party would not talk about the real quarrel. They talked "slavery." They did not themselves believe what they were saying. They used "slavery" for power, made no suggestions for solving the question. Lincoln never gave thought to a solution to slavery.

His mind never rose above private ambition and party power. He wanted to be president and "slavery" was the vehicle to carry him there.

Lincoln was lucky or shrewd in choosing his law partner. Without Herndon Lincoln might not have reached his goal. Herndon was a perfect tool to Lincoln's needs. He was smarter, better informed on all subjects, and at that time really believed in the radical program he thought Lincoln would execute. (He changed his mind later.) No other partner would have been so interested in politics, diligent in its work, yet willing to give the rewards to Lincoln. Lincoln used another asset—his connection to the elite. His mind always on the presidency, Lincoln, even before the Senate race of 1858, took a long step in that direction. Or rather Herndon did. Herndon was a personal acquaintance of the Northeastern political establishment. Lincoln ordered him to go to them, to personally assure the party leaders that Lincoln was their man, would do their bidding. Herndon did not want to go, but the loyal Lincoln lackey did yet another selfless service for the selfish man, at much trouble. The Eastern politicians readily gave him private conference, eager to learn news of the West. That connection was of immense service to Lincoln's ambition. It was a lifetime of such aggressive use of things and men that gained him his power. For Lincoln the trip was eminently successful. For Herndon it gained him nothing. He made it at his own considerable expense. Herndon did not have much money. He reported years later that Lincoln never paid him back a dime, or even showed gratitude. Once in the presidency Lincoln forgot Herndon. Lincoln knew how to use people.

At the Springfield State Fair the Abolitionists invited him to their meeting. Lincoln had given them every assurance that he was one with them. Herndon saw the danger of being outed too soon, told Lincoln to get his buggy hitched and flee the town. Lincoln excused his absence with a lie.

In 1858 the Eastern Republicans, the party power seat, gave thought to the next presidential election, to gaining the rewards so long denied them. In 1856 they had lost to the weak Buchanan;

how could they, in 1860, hope to defeat the strongest politician in the country? It seemed impossible. The eastern Republicans suggested that the Republicans make common cause with Douglas, run him on the Republican ticket. That was the surest way to win the executive office and its spoils. The idea was gaining favor until ran into a mountain—the ego of Abraham Lincoln. Lincoln was horror-struck. Such a union might help the party but it would kill Lincoln—it was Douglas's place he wanted. How history would have been changed. No war.

Lincoln sweated, and went to work. He was no rail-splitter but he sweated as a people-splitter. He told the western Republicans that the idea was a dirty scheme of the "Black Republicans" of the East. Lincoln was always willing to attack his own party when it threatened his power. He even used the opposite party's hostile label: the "Black Republicans" would cut the West out of patronage. He made the Western party leaders believe that they, not Lincoln, were in danger. It was a slick piece of work and the move to join Douglas died. "America's greatest trimmer," he could turn in a trice, from licking to kicking any adversary or ally, to serve his private interest. His life's every act a tool of ambition.

The Abolitionists' agitation was harm enough. But the real harm was done when the politicians, the men of power, took up the false issue to cover their real crimes. They set afire the race question, still burning in the national life. Lincoln was foremost among "the ambitious men" whose unprincipled conduct made the "slavery issue." The South did not introduce it, did not agitate it. Lincoln said that Southerners would enslave everybody. It was Lincoln's usurping government that enslaved everybody.

Abolitionists and Money Men

WHAT WAS MORAL ABOUT "The Secret Six"—wealthy New Englanders who in the 1854 Kansas quarrel sponsored the sociopath John Brown to go to Kansas to kill to try to make a sectional war? Not just the "Six," but the New England intellectual class supported Brown. Niggard as are intellectuals with their own money, they gave Brown money and raised more in churches. The same class backed the French Revolution. That class (the "liberals" today) do more destruction than recognized tyrants.

In 1858 they thought to force the Negroes to rise up and free themselves. They financed Brown to go to Virginia, kill, organize a slave revolt. Gerrit Smith, Dr. Samuel Gridley Howe, Thomas Wentworth Higginson, Franklin Sanborn, George Stearns, and Theodore Parker were America's first terrorists. They were wealthy and prominent, Smith one of the richest men in the country. Parker, a Herndon-Lincoln associate, was a notable Boston preacher.

The first man Brown's terrorists killed was the train depot baggage master, a free black man, Hayward Shepard. Their criminal conspiracy failed, the slaves were not interested in their scheme. The slaves were better people than Samuel Gridley Howe. They were better people than his wife, the banker's daughter, who stole William Steffe's Southern Hymn, "Glory, Glory, Hallelujah," and put the Devil's words to it, exhorting the Northern army to kill Southerners. "The Battle Hymn" is nothing Christian. The slaves were better people than Lincoln's guide, Boston's most famous preacher Theodore Parker.

Brown failed, died. Those "aristocrats" took advantage of that unbalanced man. Unsuccessful in life, he was hungry for prestige. The attention and direction of those high-placed, malicious fools rushed him to wanton murder, to death of himself and his pitiful sons. He failed but they were able to use him as a "martyr." Similarly Lincoln's invasion of Charleston Harbor failed and failure made it a success. If he had succeeded it could not have started a war.

The intellectuals of New England, including Emerson and Thoreau, applauded Brown's crimes, proving them mindless and dangerous. They made him a martyr. They were all criminals, eager murderers, guilty of treason against the United States. They demonstrated it then and proved it in making America's most vicious war—on other Americans. One New Englander, Nathaniel Hawthorne, the wisest of them all, saw their hypocrisy and the crime of their program and said that no man ever more deserved hanging than John Brown.

"The Secret Six" demonstrate that the "slavery issue" was a white man's movement, the destructive folly of white man, not a yearning for freedom by the black. The servants were happy, were normal people living a normal life, should have been left alone to let slavery end peacefully by evolution. They were as well off and frequently better off than humble laboring people in the North and Europe, as John Adams had observed to Thomas Jefferson many years before. The Abolitionists regarded them abstractly, tried to use them for revolution. Despite all the attempts to inflame them the Negroes did not rise up. They were gravely injured by the revolution forced on them by the Jacobins. It is error to say the servant was groaning under domestic servitude. The Southern black was more loyal to his society than the Northern white to his. No matter that most Abolitionists considered black people inferior in character and mind. The Abolitionists had servants; they were just not as friendly with them.

It all had to do with power and money. Where was the moral?

"Abolition" is a term like "liberal." "Liberal" seems to mean favoring liberty, when its action always is to abolish liberty. "Liberal" is really only a clever scheme of a faction to take power. "Liberals" always abuse appealing words such as "equality" and "compassion" to transfer power from individuals and localities to a government elite. "Liberal" is a nice word to disguise ambition, a method of seizing power by promising one group to use government to take something away from another group. "Liberal" is a mild word for "radical," "socialist," "Jacobin," but embodies the same hatred of private property and love of government power. "Abolition" was one department and project within the "liberals." Their method is divide and conquer. Their results are always evil. Evil origin, evil end.

The John Brown attempt to make a war of the sections frightened the South and contributed toward secession. That the sponsors of the violence were never penitent and never punished convinced the South that they would not be safe in the union. Neither secession nor war were the slaves' fault. The quarrel was not slavery. It was one faction abusing and exploiting another and covering their greed by introducing a false issue. "Slavery" was an instrument for power. Not slavery, but "abolition" gave an issue to politicians. Election of the money party caused the South to secede. Loss of Southern money caused the money party to make war. "Abolition" was dishonestly injected into an economic quarrel. "Abolition" did contribute toward secession.

The institution of slavery did not make the South secede. Slavery did not impel the South to secede, but "abolition" insult and injury did contribute to the South's fleeing Northern hate. Slavery had nothing to do with the money party making war. The Abolitionists and the South agreed on that. The money party made war because of secession, prospect of money loss. The combination of Abolitionists and money men divided the Democratic Party and the nation, scared Southerners, disturbed Northerners, and electing Lincoln.

Abolition did its greatest harm when the politicians took it up as a red herring to divert attention from their economic and power objectives. What began as an abstraction, then a fantasy of the leisured, became an instrument to power. The South seceded to escape verbal abuse and political abuse that used "Abolition" as excuse. The "abolition" movement turned political and frightened the South. It was a sign of relentless enmity. Secession led to war because the ruling party did not want to lose Southern money that left with the South. Secession caused the war. Lincoln offered guarantees of slavery, even offered the South every element of freedom except escape of tax. He demanded that the South continue to pay the tariff. Secession was the cause of America's most monstrous crime—Lincoln's war on his own country.

The money party's agitation of "slavery" produced a false fear in the Northern mind and a valid one in the Southern. They provoked the Northern people to fear trouble from distant blacks. It never happened. They alarmed the abused Southern people to fear attack by whites. That happened in catastrophe.

For their private gain, the money party disrupted a necessary, routine piece of public business, the admission of a new state. They fabricated a shameless lie that "slavery" was a peril to be suffered by voting Democratic; a peril from which they would be saved by voting Republican. By agitating that false issue they produced fear enough to empower Lincoln and his party to lead the country to the "safety" of America's bloodiest and most destructive war. It was an act of treason. For which they were rewarded.

Slavery was two different subjects in the two sections. The Northern people were not hostile to the South, they looked upon the Abolitionists as foolish, idle trouble makers, and upon the politicians as just that—politicians. The national quarrel was not between the Southern people and the Northern people, it was between the Southern people and the Northern politicians.

The politicians were shameless. On every question in Congress where North disagreed with South, the Northern politicians would declare the irrelevancy: "You are slave drivers." John Quincy Adams avenged himself on the Southern Democrats that had ended his presidency. He stayed busy during his long post-presidency tenure in Congress, concocting schemes to punish Democrats, introducing a continual flow of anti-South petitions. Money party politicians could not say, "Vote for me because I want the control of a new state," or "We want to subsidize our industry with Southern tariff and Northern Internal Improvements." They had to give some reason for running for office. Slavery was unrelated, but it was exciting and distracting. For a Northern politician it was a perfect issue—risk-free. One did not have to be specific, just indict the other party as "slaveholders." They did not make the "slavery issue" to make war, but to make money.

Several factions in the North were working against the South. Adams's group were the New England Whigs, descended from the Federalists. Their rancor at losing to the Democrats still burned. Even the Democrats of the North joined the attack. Van Buren's faction, which had its own contingent of New York money men, after defeat by the Southern Polk, joined the anti-South faction. Polk had opposed government spending. The money party attacked him rather than attending their proper duty of office. They wanted the Democrats' place and patronage. The issue was not principle but place.

Meanwhile, the money party was growing. To the New England and New Jersey textile producers, the Vermont wool merchants, and the Pennsylvania iron men, was added in the 1850s a strong corps of flourishing new Midwestern industrialists. Detroit and Chicago grew from villages into large and busy cities within a few short years. And the money party had what it always had—Wall Street investors in government bonds and private banks fostered by the government. The money party had grown stronger, more aggressive, and more than ever determined that the purpose of the Federal Government was to aid them in gathering wealth—and that the South was the major obstacle in their way.

The rhetoric of New England party becoming ever louder and nastier in denunciation of the barbarous South which must be eradicated from the American story. The party became increasingly dishonest and increasingly bellicose. Using the "slavery" tool, the Republicans circulated Mrs. Stowe's imaginary, untrue novel. They paid for three hundred thousand copies of Hinton Rowan Helper's book Helper's book to inflame the North. The latter was a project of powerful Senator John Sherman, brother of William. Their war, later, was just politics. Neither Sherman cared about the Negro, both cared about power.

The Abolitionists declared that the businessmen cared nothing for abolition or for slaves, only for money. The businessmen affirmed it. Many people of Boston, at the very moment of secession, were actively opposing the activities of the

Abolitionists. The Abolitionists themselves had turned from violence. In Boston nobody made any connection between slavery and secession, or slavery and war. The Abolitionists, Howe, Sumner, Phillips, at first said let the South go. They censured the money men for their selfish motives.

For the money party the real Kansas-Nebraska issue was to use "slavery" to gain states for their party and office for themselves.

Slavery was unrelated to statehood. "Slavery" agitation in Kansas-Nebraska was a false issue. The red herring stank, but a stink draws attention. "Slavery" was a tool to gain notice, for Abraham Lincoln to use to rise off the dusty sofa in his hated law office and pursue a seat in the White House. And use "principle" to serve ambition. He would drag that red herring along the campaign trail.

Presidents Pierce and Buchanan, though Northerners, were part of the Northern Democrat group favorable to the South. That is what infuriated their Republican political opponents. An intact Democratic Party, drawing votes North and South, would forever deny the money men the national executive power. The "slavery" tumult succeeded. It did more than cover their greed. It won elections, confused the electorate, estranged President Buchanan and his party's candidate, Douglas. It split the anti-Republican vote into three parts, guaranteeing that any Republican would win.

The territory argument over Kansas-Nebraska is the perfect illustration of what politics is and does. Abraham Lincoln was willing to make, from nothing, all the Kansas-Nebraska trouble in order to make him a career. It was indeed the making of the career of Abraham Lincoln. Without Kansas-Nebraska he would have died unknown, unable to make the war that made his fame. In the drama known as "Territorial Expansion" his role was an artificial piece of play-acting. He put his private reward above the common good. The publicly declared issue was not the real one. The real reason was money, party rivalry, factions fighting for power. Foreign observers saw the truth. From the British Foreign Secretary in Whitehall to Karl Marx in the British Museum, there was agreement, the real issue was that the Southern economy wanted relief, the Northern politicians wanted power.

Many Southerners did not like Douglas's position: the Constitution prohibited Congress from intruding into state affairs, specifically slavery. If Northerners could settle in new territory, it was not fair to suddenly decree that Southerners did not have that right. The precedent could be used to block Southern farmers out of other new lands. The non-Democrat-Party politicians took a third position: They said that Congress could exclude Southerners from all territories before they became states, that even local voting was wrong.

Douglas could not satisfy everybody, he would lose some of at least one part—North or South—of the electorate, maybe some of both. Voters who had eluded the money party for so long would be pried loose from the Democrats. Lincoln succeeded—he hurt Douglas in both sections. If the Kansas-Nebraska issue had not been hoisted, Douglas would have been unbeatable. Douglas's opponents were a group wanting what Douglas had—Office: place, emoluments, power. They now had a vehicle to carry them. Lincoln could make "slavery agitation" a "principle" and ride it to glory. His act was treason. Slavery agitation gained him notice to gain the presidency. And then commit the worst treason—war.

Lincoln's Election

ABRAHAM LINCOLN WAS ELECTED PRESIDENT by manipulating a public event to serve himself. Principle never had a hand in it. Kansas-Nebraska statehood should have been a simple routine transaction. A statesman would have left it alone. The politician seized it, put it to his use. His fellows said that was his way. Each new state would add power to one party or the other. That was the real quarrel, the real reason behind Northern opposition to Kentucky statehood, Louisiana Purchase, Missouri, Gadsden Purchase, Texas, Mexican War, California, and Kansas-Nebraska. They used "slavery" to divert attention from the real issue—power. The real issue to them in the 19th century was to take the place of the Democrats. That was not an issue to the voters.

Lincoln posed himself as caring for the slave. His colleagues called him singularly indifferent to the condition or needs of others. His false definition, labeling blacks as victims and whites as villains, has, because he won a war, become an accepted, permanent, public definition, creating ill-will that still poisons the nation. Later Lincolns, to serve their power greed, are still using that hypocrisy.

Without that false issue, Stephen A. Douglas and the Democrats would have won the presidency. The Republican Party made a political war to win power, then Lincoln made a killing war to hold it. So much suffering forced on so many millions to benefit a few hundred. The business party readily rejected the restraints of the Constitution for government booty.

Lincoln's drive for the presidency was of two separate parts, one gaining the nomination, the other gaining the general election. For the general election it was mere theater, he had been performing the actor's role for years. But first he had to gain the party nomination. Whatever Republican won the nomination would probably win the election. The election was a matter of show business. The nomination was a matter of monkey business—maneuver and manipulation.

Henry Whitney was Lincoln's political intimate, or as close an intimate as anybody could be with the dissembling Lincoln. He said:

"Truth requires me to concede that the proximate cause of Mr. Lincoln's nomination was adroit and astute political skill and management at the convention. The ultimate and remote causes were his political genius. He was inspired on May 29 or thereabouts (1856) to compete for the high exaltation."

Lincoln was relentless. No other aspirant started campaigning so early, worked at it so long, gave such attention to detail. He benefited from rare luck, but he gave the chase rare diligence and cunning. His maneuvers started years before the elections. Before the Senate race, looking to the presidency, he sent Herndon east to assure the party leaders that he was their agent. Lincoln never did do much work. He was labeled a lazy youth, a lackadaisical lawyer, and an indolent president. There was one kind of work he did do—office hunting. Was it work, or sport? He wrote thousands of letters, traveled thousands of miles.

The "slavery issue" did its dirty work. The public was confused, the Democrats were confounded, lying helpless in the water, so injured that the Republican nomination was more important than the general election. Whoever won the Republican nomination would win the election. Gaining the party nomination was an entirely different operation from the general election. There was not even the pretense of "ideals," "morals," or "principles" declared so piously in public elections. Election is won by fooling the people, nomination is won by bribing the politicians.

Whoever won the Republican nomination would win the election. The party nomination was a tournament, a chase for national booty they would all share, first prize going to the wiliest or the luckiest. Taking advantage, political opportunism—that was Lincoln's talent. Campaigning since 1856, he and his organization had traveled widely, started recruiting delegates years before his rivals had begun to think of it. There was no Republican leader, however small, that Lincoln had not noted, studied, approached, used by individual utility.

Telling nobody, he bought German language newspapers and labeled Seward, his rival for the nomination, anti-immigrant. Lincoln took the German vote, greatly increased by immigration to the Midwest in the 1850s. Seward, who never knew what Lincoln was doing to him, was hurt more by Lincoln than by the rival party. Seward had committed the error of saying there was an "irrepressible conflict" brewing between the sections. It was no more than campaign rhetoric delivered to excite the upper North, to make them believe slavery was a menace to them. Lincoln was saying the same things but in safer words. It was a gift to Lincoln. He made the most of it, hung those words on Seward and exaggerated their harm to the party's public image. Lincoln had his claque whisper in the ears of Republican nominating delegates that Seward could not be elected. Lincoln was working with the Democrats against his own party fellow.

Lincoln boxed out the other candidates. He was able to spread a suspicion that Seward was a warmonger. The fact was just opposite. Seward sincerely liked Jefferson Davis. Later, he opposed Lincoln's desire to make war. If Seward had been elected there would have been no war. How fatal is fate. Lincoln overcame Seward by "adroit" but not honest political maneuvers. Lincoln hurt Seward before the convention. In the convention he applied the *coup de grace*. Seward was ambushed, overwhelmed by the aggressive Lincoln, playing by his own rules of conduct. Lincoln printed counterfeit tickets that excluded Seward's supporters, he intruded his noisy intimidating claque into the hall, orchestrated the proceedings and crowd behavior.

The "slavery issue" did its dirty work. The public were confused, the Democrats were confounded, lying helpless in the water, so injured that the Republican nomination was more important than the general election. Gaining the party nomination was an entirely different operation from the general election. There was not even the pretense of "ideals," "morals," or "principles" declared so piously in public elections. Election is won by fooling the people, nomination is won by bribing the politicians.

Whoever won the Republican nomination would win the election. The party nomination was a tournament, a chase for national booty they would all share, first prize going to the wiliest or the luckiest. Taking advantage, political opportunism—that was Lincoln's talent. Campaigning since 1856, he and his organization had traveled widely, started recruiting delegates years before his rivals had begun to think of it. There was no Republican leader, however small, that Lincoln had not noted, studied, approached, used by individual utility.

When Lincoln was introduced to the convention, John Hanks appeared with him, carrying some fence rails. He shouted that Lincoln had split them as a youth. That of the man whose neighbors said, "He split fewer rails than anybody in the county." That display, supporting Lincoln's "modesty" claim, was a theatrical success, giving the party newspapers an image they could impose on the hapless electorate—the "honest country boy," the "common man," so different from the rich eastern Republicans. In fact, he was a courthouse lounger, a slick lawyer, a hack politician. The performance was an act, rehearsed beforetime. It is impossible that the real country boy, John Hanks, had any more to do with the show than carry the rails. Lincoln was the showman. Where he got the rails is anybody's guess. It is certain he found the idea before Hanks. Poor John, the only one of Lincoln's kin who voted for him.

Lincoln climbed up not by virtue, but by zeal. And luck. A rare series of favorable events. The factors that made his success were merely and strictly political. No candidate ever had such luck as Lincoln. A timely economic recession was blamed on the incumbent party (as in 1932). Lincoln's previous failures to win office shielded him from an identifying record. He had a passive partner, for years willing to run the office, do the work and let Lincoln campaign. His partner just happened to be associate of both the eastern Republicans and the Abolitionists, giving Lincoln personal contact. The nominating convention just happened to be in his state.

More important to his ambition, President Buchanan turned against Douglas, used his power to defeat Douglas. That alone should be enough to give victory to the opposite party. There was a final one, making it certain that any Republican would win—the opposition split; split not just into two but into three parts. The Democrats guaranteed the victory of their opponent. Lincoln's victory was handed to him. Even so, it was not overwhelming.

In 1860 the looming prospect of Abraham Lincoln as president threw the long-apprehensive South into alarm. They anticipated disaster. They knew Lincoln would hurt them, the only question was just how much. How far would he go? They predicted he would stop at nothing. Before the election Lincoln scoffed at the suggestion that for power his party would commit violence. He said this not to reassure the South but to allay Northern doubts about his party. In time his violence exceeded the South's wildest nightmares and did not confine itself to the South.

Once nominated, Lincoln told his wife he would be the next president of the United States.

The actual institution of slavery never interested Lincoln. He was on the side of slavery in the Matson case. He traveled all the way to Kentucky to contest ownership of family slaves. When his father-in-law died he was a lawyer for the older Todd children in settling their father's estate, selling slaves and taking his share of the money. He agreed with Illinois laws to exclude Negroes and mulattoes from voting, from holding office, and from migrating to Illinois. He enjoyed the dowry of one slaveholder, the hospitality of many. A lengthy visit in the home of a slaveholder saved him from depression. He had no interest in slavery until he found "slavery."

He was America's first entirely sectional major candidate for president. His party had shamelessly driven the South out of the common territories, had parasitized the South far worse than the British, even the Romans, had parasitized their colonies. Lincoln had arrayed the North to hate the South. What right did he have to control the South when he did not get a single vote there? Is that government by consent of the governed? What kind of Democracy is it when a man for whom the people refused to vote is forced upon them by armed invasion which takes their lives?

Abraham Lincoln, to get elected, broadcast that black people going north was a peril. They would compete with white labor. That lie would not impress the Southerners who were used to living and working with Negroes, but it was effective with the immigrants such as the Germans, Irish and English who had just come to the United States because they were unemployed at home. The lie frightened them. He was wrong in two ways: the black people would not be going north in any numbers, he knew it. And they would not be a peril if they had. He knew that, too. The money party claimed to oppose Southern migration on moral grounds—"slavery." Their claimed objection was a lie and a subterfuge.

Agitating "slavery" would attract voters from many factions: Abolitionists, money men, western settlers, immigrants from Europe, and the remote, ordinary citizens.

1. Abolitionists. Idle troublemakers, leisured intellectuals, Humanist Jacobins, Puritan hypocrites. "Slavery" agitation was the basis of their drive for power. Hawthorne said those "weird people" lusted to rule the world if they had to kill it.

2. Northern money men who wanted to keep the rival Southern farmer party from gaining another state.

3. Western settlers did not want Negroes moving into their area, for reasons both racial and economic. It was not slavery they opposed, but Negro migration.

4. Immigrants from Europe. Alarmed by the slavery agitation, they were told Negroes coming north was a "peril." Lincoln said that the South if allowed north would enslave them. To the numerous immigrants the South was unknown and seemed alien and threatening.

5. Ordinary Northerners everywhere. The largest group of all, they opposed the idea of slavery on principle, in abstract

philanthropy. Everybody did. The politicians would take advantage of the good will of everybody.

Those factions presented a crop that the Republicans could cultivate by planting the "slavery issue." They were planting tares, an evil seed, but it could fatten the party. Slavery, the institution, was irrelevant to the quarrel. "Slavery, the issue," was a dishonest weapon of political war.

The North was unconcerned because essentially unaffected by the furor over "the expansion of slavery." They did not vote for Lincoln because of any affection for him, he was just another politician—but their politician. Whatever he might do to hurt the far-off Southerners did not bother them. They did not love the Negro or hate the white, they just liked their own interest. War was not on their minds. It was business-as-usual for the North.

New Englanders and their western cousins saw an irresistible opportunity to return to power and thwart the hated South. To them slaves were distant abstractions. Personal danger of war was not feared—wealth and distance would keep that away. They did not see Lincoln as the South did, or as the West did. They saw themselves finally gaining control of the Federal power they had been so long denied. In earlier times, their Federalist-Whig Party always had some Southern members. Now, for the first time, it was totally Northern. They now had no brake on their power. That frightened the South but not the North—they saw no danger in Lincoln. New England did not respect Lincoln but he was of their party. He would benefit their section, their party, their politicians, and their business. Charles Francis Adams was appalled by Lincoln's crass, cynical political nature, but it did not stop him from accepting Lincoln's appointment to the Court of Saint James.

Beforehand, the South knew Lincoln and feared him. He and his party had abused government power to parasitize the South for fifty years. To cover it they had added the dishonest slavery agitation. His anti-farmer party that had been able to take so much when it had only a Congressional majority, would now have the Executive Office. For the first time the president would be a man who represented one narrow faction only, one region, one class, the urban capitalists. Lincoln was not only of the hostile party but allied to its violent, anti-South wing—the "Radical Republicans." He deliberately polarized his country to drive Northern voters away from the "dangerous" Democratic Party. His past actions and recent statements had been bellicose.

Notwithstanding the sureness of success, Lincoln was seen to be nervous at election time, calming his anxiety by drinking beer and pitching horseshoes. He won, his victory easy but thin. Despite all his shrewd maneuvers and favoring public events, Lincoln still was elected president by the lowest margin in American history—39.9% of the votes. In ten states he did not get a single vote. George Washington asked citizens to vote for individual virtuous men to represent them and for those representatives to select others—a republic, not a democracy. He begged his country to not make parties. Party politics is what put Lincoln in office.

Lincoln was not popular. He won not much more vote than Fremont had in 1856. In the 1860 election, total vote was 4.7 million. Lincoln received 1.8 million votes, the other candidates received 2.8 million votes, a million more votes than he did. His vote in Illinois was 50%. In the Midwest Lincoln's majority was only 6,600, and German refugees from their 1848 revolution were responsible for that. A change of one vote in 20 in his own region would have beat him.

Lincoln would fail to carry his own district. Not a single Lincoln would vote for him. Only one Hanks. His peers around Springfield did not vote for him. But, enough strangers did to make him president.

He had devoted his life to pursuit of power. He had no interest but politics. He defeated his political rivals because he gave more attention to political affairs than they did. He saw what was necessary to win and did it. The elements of politics are public notice, attention-gathering speeches, and organized maneuver. He won office because: he was the most earnest seeker, an effective speaker, and lucky. His victory was made because of a rare combination of fortuitous events: the incumbent party was injured by national depression, suicidal splits of opposite party, fortunate happenings in his own party, massive immigration. He did not win for any reason of virtue. If Lincoln had been an unselfish man he would have been a statesman, not a politician. For he abused truth to stigmatize part of his country and later victimize all of it.

President Abraham Lincoln would injure America more than any other man, or measure, or act, ever done within or without its borders. He would do more damage to America than all its other miscreants combined. He would do more harm to his own people than all foreign rulers together. But, he cured his lifelong itch.

STEPHEN A. DOUGLAS FORETELLS THE DISASTER OF LINCOLN'S RULE

Failure to elect Stephen A. Douglas as president doomed to oblivion a federative republic and millions of lives. That election made an unnecessary, horrible war, an imperial government, and from political dirt, a clay god. Douglas would never have brought those horrors if he had been president. He would have been president but that a few evil men of ambition injected the "slavery" poison into the body politic. If he had been president the nation would have been spared, its people remaining alive and free.

In 1800, Thomas Jefferson's agricultural party decisively defeated the New England money party. The money party took it hard. The farmer party held the presidency until 1824. The money party won it for one term. In 1828, the farmer party, under Andrew Jackson, again decisively defeated the money party. The money party took it hard. That was the end of the Federalist Party. Its dregs seethed at loss of the executive power, but were soothed by control of Congress and the other-party presidents who acquiesced to their policies. Jackson was a Southerner and a farmer, but he was also naive, subject to flattery, and fiercely willful. The money party manipulated him to force their measures that so injured the South. They doubled the tariff. The South protested. The money party had the effrontery to blame Southern tariff protest on "slavery" when the president who executed their money policy for them was himself a slaveholder.

The Democratic Party was a national party, had voters in all the states. The money party, now called Whig, was regional, located mostly in the North. In 1848 the Whig Party ran and won a slaveholder for president. Lincoln worked hard for Taylor, accused the Democratic opposition of the crime of anti-slavery. He said it was wrong to inject the slavery issue into politics. In 1852 the money party was defeated by the Democrats. That was the end of the Whigs. The money party was effectually denied the Executive Office since 1800. They took it hard.

The Whig dregs formed a new party. They were the same crowd, the non-Democrats, a gang looking for power. The Whig Party was made by the dregs of an exhausted Federalist Party. The Republican Party was made by the dregs of an exhausted Whig Party. The Republicans in 1854 seized, brandished, the "slavery issue." It was safe, there was no slavery in their own area. The most ambitious of them all, Abraham Lincoln, took up "slavery" to make him "a full-time candidate for the presidency." To raise him from oblivion to glory. He saw what was operating against Douglas: Mathematics. Adding immigrants. Dividing the Democrats on "slavery." It was math. He called it moral. The Republicans offered their most divisive speaker the 1858 nomination for Senate. Lincoln took it gladly, he was really after the presidency.

Douglas had problems. Republican "slavery" agitation was splitting the party, alienating Northern and Southern Democrats. His own party's president, James Buchanan, angry at Douglas, was working to hurt Douglas politically. And, the Van Buren wing of the Democrats were angry at the party for denying him a second nomination.

The election contained two elements. One was fact—Douglas's difficult position in the splintering Democratic Party. The Democrats were a party of North and South. Sectional estrangement would hurt him. The second element was fiction—the Republican Party fabricating a "slavery issue." They had nothing else but the true story, greed. Divide and conquer. No matter its result. Pity the real victim—the people.

In the Northwest—Ohio, Indiana, Michigan, Illinois, and Iowa—there was a particular circumstance. The original Southern farmers settling in those states were being followed by large numbers of immigrants from the North, and from England, Ireland, and Germany. They knew nothing about Negroes, or slavery. They did not want Negroes, slave or free, to come into their territory. Lincoln stimulated that fear.

Lincoln made his "House Divided" speech on June 17, 1858. It was not factual, only a fable to frighten the North: The South was evil. The Republican Party would save them from that evil. He wanted to polarize the regions, sow discord, split the Democrats, make the Northern and Western Democrats leave the party of the agricultural South. To win, his party must break the national character of the Democratic Party.

So Lincoln called on the Bible: "A house divided against itself cannot stand. The nation cannot endure half slave and half free. It will eventually become all one thing or all the other." That was nonsense. It was worse than nonsense, it was untrue. It was politics. It was effective. "House Divided" demonstrates his practice. Quote the Bible for its impressive tone, make a slogan of it, and disregard the meaning. He scared the people with a false alarm. Alarm was his purpose. His fellows told him that that threat would so frighten the North that they would elect him president. The nation had stood divided and healthy for two hundred fifty years, and would continue to stand if he would leave it in peace. The South was no threat to the North. Lincoln knew it.

He lied in saying that there was an evil conspiracy among the Democrats: the moral Chief Justice Roger Taney, the honest President Pierce, the genuinely-concerned President Buchanan, and the straight-talking Douglas. Lincoln worked up a conspiracy tale, his practice in the court room and on the stump. "Roger, Frank, James, and Steve" had conspired to force slavery upon the country. He evaded facts, spoke agitating generalities, slogans, meaningless metaphysics. He chose words mystical, religious, Biblical. Like all demagogues he did not speak to a specific question, but used public events to confuse and inflame for his profit. His colleagues, even his party fellows, said he was never candid, even his private talk was for self-gain. "Honest" Abe was no more than a party label. Lincoln's speech was artful agitation, a threat to scare, to divide, a falsehood, for his country impious, for him safely pious.

On July 9, 1858, Douglas responded with a different kind of speech. He gave a factual and practical analysis of the question. He named the problem and the proper solution. He said the people in Maine should be allowed to make their own decisions on how to conduct their business, and the people of Virginia and Kansas to do likewise. The states were sovereign, and the central government had no business dominating them.

Douglas said Lincoln was wrong in two propositions: The "House Divided" speech was a denial that the nation could endure half slave and half non-slave. It was no more than an attempt to frighten the people. It meant that Lincoln would have conflict without end until slavery was either spread throughout the nation or abolished throughout the nation. It meant "a war of sections, a war of the North against the South—a war of extermination to be persisted in relentlessly until either North or South is subdued."

Douglas said that such forced uniformity was not necessary, not right, not desirable. It was not even possible to attain what Lincoln claimed, but would create never-ending discord. Each state was sovereign over its internal affairs, delegating to the Federal Government only certain "specific powers which were general and national." Lincoln either did not understand or did not desire that "fundamental principle." Douglas uttered a powerful truth: "Uniformity is the parent of despotism. All over the world." Let Lincoln's idea be followed and "you have destroyed the greatest safeguard which our institutions have erected to protect the rights of the citizens. To achieve what Lincoln would bring, uniformity, could be accomplished only at the price of taking away the sovereignty of the states and rights of the people. It would give to us a government where all the power is taken by the consolidated empire, and Congress would be vested with the plenary power to make all the policy regulations, domestic and local laws, uniform throughout the republic."

The superiority of Douglas over Lincoln is demonstrated in Douglas's prophecy of what Lincoln would accomplish: "Then the states will be all one or all the other, all slave or all free. We will have all things the same everywhere, uniformity in all things, local and domestic by the authority of the Federal Government. But, when you obtain that uniformity, you will have converted these thirty-two sovereign, independent states into one consolidated empire with uniformity, the uniformity of despotism, reigning triumphant throughout the length and breadth of the land."

After showing that Lincoln would destroy freedom, Douglas turned to Lincoln's second position, Lincoln's attack on the Supreme Court's Dred Scott decision. "Lincoln has asked the people to disobey the Court. Lincoln's doctrine is to block the decisions of the court and let the law be determined by a Republican Party caucus. The only doctrine that would maintain our freedoms is to observe the Constitution, respect and maintain the courts, and observe the laws.

Douglas was specific and honest. "The citizens must preserve the purity of government as well as race, and there must be neither physical nor political force. The dire results of such policies are apparent in the countries to the south of the United States. The only safe policy is to accord to dependent races all privileges society's safety will permit." That was Douglas's "Popular Sovereignty." Local government, self-government, government by the people. Contrast that with Lincoln's consolidated power. Abraham Lincoln believed in fortune tellers. Stephen Douglas was a perfect fortune teller. "*Sic transit libertas.*" Thus passes away liberty.

Abraham Lincoln's War

"War is the worst of human terrors. No decent man would, no Christian could, make a war."

—LEO TOLSTOY

"As long as mankind shall accord more applause to their destroyers than to their benefactors, those characters seeking glory will seek war."

—EDWARD GIBBON

"The man who shall inaugurate war will be the greatest murderer that ever disgraced the form of man, will go down to his grave covered with the curses of Heaven and the cries of thousands of widows and orphans."

—OREGON SENATOR JOEL LANE, MARCH 1861

THOUGH THEY DENY IT, HISTORIANS attribute war to altruism, Lincoln's war more than any. War is made by the opposite of altruism, by pride, the chief sin. War, the ultimate horror, is the ultimate expression of self-interest, worldly power, the Devil's Proposition.

The most self-loving of the Springfield lawyers made a war because he loved himself more than he loved his neighbor.

On Tuesday, November 6, 1860, Abraham Lincoln was elected president. The country was divided. Its eighty-year regional conflict had risen to a high peak. The party that caused the conflict by intruding a false issue, afflicting the nation with an irrelevant, exciting subject, had taken the presidency. What kind of man was the new president? His country called for a statesman. His party called for a partisan—the Democrats were divided but not dead.

The money party, able to gain government preferment even when the presidency was held by the opposite party, now had won the Executive Office. Abraham Lincoln was the complete party man, a lifelong servant of Northern economic interest. He had promised to raise the tariff to its highest level and to promote all money party measures that fed it with Southern money.

Before taking presidential power he had to endure a four-month wait in Springfield. He later told friends, "That was the most anxious period of my life." One would suppose that his anxiety was for the welfare of his country, for the happiness of the people subject to his power. What would he do? Would he serve his country or his party? War being the worst of human terrors, surely the president-elect would exert his utmost to prevent war. Certainly not make one.

During that period he did what he always did—politics. Not statesmanship. He occupied his time in huddling with his party and dispensing patronage. Publicly he practiced a purposed silence.

General-in-Chief Winfield Scott wanted him to made assurances of peace. "The Union is at the mercy of the President-elect even before he is inaugurated. His silence may be fatal." Lincoln made no answer, refused any meeting, ordered his party to refuse negotiation. Thousands of entreaties—petitions, letters, personal visits—begged him to make some assurance to the South that he would not hurt them. He refused to do so. His cold rejection sent some Northern peace pleaders away in tears.

The Republicans in Congress, inflamed with access to power, openly taunted the South. Even before South Carolina seceded they threatened to make war, to seize the Southern ports and collect the tariff.

Southerners feared that the Republicans, who had already excited, even committed violence, sponsored John Brown, insulted Southerners as criminals, and threatened war, would soon make a real war upon the South. When the Southern Congressman tried to protest Northern threats, the Northerners openly laughed at them.

There was ample evidence that the South needed reassurance and would respond to kindness. It did not come from Lincoln. He refused to even talk about it. He told irrelevant jokes, exerted his influence to block all negotiation. Officially, Lincoln had no power. Practically, he had plenty of power, inheritor of the purse and the sword, enough to have made peace. Most of his party did not desire war, but the powers of his party, wealthy financiers and manufacturers, urged it and began increasing the pressure on Lincoln. He had always followed their direction. General Halleck, Lincoln's chief-of-staff during the war, said later that Lincoln always eventually did what the radicals directed.

Abraham Lincoln was described by his closest associates as selfish, self-absorbed, self-esteeming, shallow. All he knew was politics. He was a party politician. Nothing more. His character and his record told what he would do. He had no understanding, no principle; he had no philosophical or religious affection for peace. He told his associates that he would make war if the South seceded. In December he told Chase and Trumbull that in case of secession, "I'll make a cemetery of the South." He had endorsed war in conversation with Herndon in 1859. Compromise would defeat the Republican agenda.

On December 20, 1860, South Carolina seceded. For sixty years the money party, by whatever name, had threatened to secede, had praised disunion. One house of legislature in Massachusetts voted secession, the other would have but for the sudden end of the 1812 war. All the New England states had cited the right of secession. So had Lincoln. What changed their minds? Now possessing the Executive Office, they demanded war to prevent secession. None of the Democrats wanted war. The Republican Party was a sectional party but the Republican voters did not want war. The voters were not the party. The party's rulers are the party. The businessmen who wanted money and their political agents who wanted power were the party.

President Buchanan wanted peace, and might have had it but for lack of nerve to countermand the occupation of Sumter. He could have evacuated the few troops there. That would have ended the opportunity for the Republicans to use the fort as excuse for war. Nobody could have stopped him. The Republicans would have howled in rage for depriving them of that tool. They would have looked for and doubtless found another excuse, but it would have been harder, more obvious.

The nation could have had peace if the Republicans had allowed it. How history would have been changed. But better to kill the people than the party. Republicans were harshly attacking Buchanan for not starting military action against the South, but Buchanan could have stood them down. He could have appealed to the people, asserted in the strongest terms that the Republicans would make war and the people would suffer. He could have declared that war was unthinkable. Countless Northerners and border state people had already made that point and would continue saying so until the day Lincoln invaded Charleston Harbor. If Buchanan had pronounced that there was no legal way to force the states back, that war would kill mothers' sons, he would have made the money party's task harder. That is why their agent later said, "The time between the election and inauguration was the most anxious period of my life," meaning that he feared the matter would be settled before he could take power and decide it to his party's advantage.

Buchanan missed a critical opportunity. He would have been cursed but have saved the American people. Northern majority sentiment favored a national referendum on the Crittenden Compromise. Politicians in the North said the people wanted peace, that any vote for peace would be supported by large majorities in their states. Slavery was no issue. Lincoln discarded it and promised not to bother slavery. Slavery was not the real issue, anyway. Lincoln and the New England politicians blocked every effort for peace.

From November 1860 to March 1861 the Republicans lost the one Congressional election and most municipal elections in the North. The party man had reason for anxiety. Lincoln saw the obvious—the Northern people were not wedded to the Republican Party. Before he was inaugurated all he could do was use his potential power to block settlement. He did exert that power to his utmost. Lincoln's intention was clear to the South. He would attempt military coercion. Douglas predicted it. So did Buchanan. Douglas exerted every power he possessed to rouse Congress to resist the executive.

If the North learned Lincoln meant war, they would turn against him. He was carefully building circumstances that would support his intention—empower his party and kill his country. He devoted his time to the party, not to the people. Before his inauguration he disdained talk, made irrelevant, impertinent, even vulgar, responses to entreaties, calculated to block agreement, alienate the South, and instruct the North that the South was "enemy." The South anticipated what was coming but still made every effort for harmony. Earnest and anxious conciliation attempts were made. President Buchanan's entreaty to join him in a bipartisan settlement was refused. He killed the Crittenden Compromise that would have laid the matter to rest forever. The Northern people wanted the strife settled peaceably; the Republican elite blocked it.

An independent South would end the money men's monopolies. The South might even start manufacturing. The prospect of monopoly loss enraged the monopolists. They had another problem. They would also lose their "issue." To cover their work they had made a "moral" issue—"slavery." That issue was dead and gone now, whether the South were in or out of the union. That would leave the party with their money but without voters. They would be back where they were for the last sixty years: the sections re-united, the Democrats again taking the executive office every four years and many state elections every year.

———

Lincoln's inaugural address made it clear that there was no other issue but the tariff. He promised the South anything they wanted, independence on every other element, but those prospects of loss disturbed the money party and made secession unacceptable. The North would not allow the second American secession for the same reason the British would not allow the first. The same old tax issue that had for so long and so cruelly injured the South and enriched the North. The same old tax issue that had been the only cause of the disagreement and strife between North and South, even before the Constitution was signed.

It was money. It was the power of tax. The United States Congress was now dominated by Abraham Lincoln's party. The Radical Republicans, America's first Jacobins. Republicans, no longer restrained by the Southern agriculturists in Congress, enacted the "Morrill Tariff." It was the highest tariff America had ever known, the world's highest: 50% for most, 60% for some, imported articles. The inefficient Northern industry would now be completely protected from the cheaper and better European goods.

Then came the climax: On March 11, 1861, the Confederate Congress enacted its tariff. The Confederate States of America, true to their principle of free trade, set the tax rate on imported goods at 5%. *When Jefferson Davis signed that bill, he was signing the death warrant on the South.* Free trade in North America would undermine Northern industry, finance, trade, and shipping. The Northern economic monopoly would be finished.

For the first time in the history of the Union the money men would have to start paying taxes. The South would no longer be present to finance the central government which the money men controlled. The money men would lose the cheap source of raw materials; that is, the South would not be bound to the New England bankers, would turn to other sources, European finance, eager to do business with them. The South would again be able to swap its farm products for European manufactures, to their mutual advantage. The subsidy of Northern business called "internal improvements" would be lost forever. Worse still, the South might turn the tables on the money men and put a tariff on Mississippi River commerce. The Confederates had specifically declared that they would never put a toll on the river. They had officially promised "free trade." But the New England money men feared the South would be as big liars as they were.

Free trade would not kill the North. The rich Yankees would remain rich, but their monopoly would be gone. Such a condition was unacceptable to the money men. "Better kill every last man, woman, and child in the South than let them get away with this." So said the *New York Times* after they saw the Southern tariff. A Boston newspaper said:

> "Trade is the motive operating to prevent the return of the seceded states. They are now for commercial independence. If the Southern Confederation is allowed to carry out a policy of only nominal duty on imports the business of the chief Northern cities will be seriously injured. The difference is so great between the tariff of the Union and that of the Confederate States that the entire Northwest will purchase their goods at New Orleans rather than New York. The manufacturing interests of the North will suffer when the imports shift to the South because of the low duties. The government of the United States must prevent such an event taking place."

For the money men there was only one choice—war. Nobody connected secession to slavery. Nobody connected slavery to war. Nobody connected secession to war except the businessmen. Loss of Southern money would reduce the money men to mere affluence. Loss of the "slavery issue" would require Republican politicians to go back home and go to work. The die was cast. If they could not hold power by consent of the governed, they would have to take it by force. It is called usurpation.

They went to the president of the United States and demanded war. The president was America's premier party politician. No man in history has ever been more of a party man than Abraham Lincoln. Without war his own party would destroy him. They would have his head. The alternative was to serve his country instead of his party and maintain peace. For the party, and the president of that party, it was either "Them or Us." Better "Them." Lincoln did what he always did, he didn't even have to think, he went with his party. It was easy. Let anybody who thinks it was hard for Lincoln to start a war come forth and show evidence of it.

He started the war.

The tariff law of 1787 was the first shot of the war of 1861. The North shot; the South was the target. The New England money men did love money. Hawthorne said so.

Lincoln did what he had to do. To his cabinet he suggested war. They at first opposed it. Considering their character and later conduct, the reason was not principle but policy, not Christian love but fear that the Northern public would not accept it.

There is not a shred of evidence that Lincoln worried then or ever over the horrors of his war. Rather, he warmed to the power of it. Herndon said the only suffering he ever pitied was his own. Statements of his associates like Whitney and Herndon and of Lincoln himself demonstrate his indifference to anybody else's suffering, including that which he himself brought—his war.

Raphael Semmes wrote that one of the bitterest disappointments of his life was the response of substantial Northern leaders to Lincoln's war. Men whom Semmes trusted, men of principle he thought, men who despised Lincoln, men who promised to oppose Lincoln—as soon as Lincoln started the war those men reversed their stand and toadied his favor. Such are the uses of power.

The devious Edwin Stanton despised, insulted, and fought Lincoln before the war. Once the war was started, the former Lincoln reviler changed sides, joined Lincoln's party and his cabinet. Lincoln was known for his policy of giving offices to his opponents, thereby removing their opposition, converting them and their faction to his support. Benjamin Butler had supported John C. Breckinridge. When Lincoln started the war Butler changed parties and adhered to Lincoln, who made him a general and one of the cruelest of the Yankee officers. The Blair family, former Democrats, were the first to press Lincoln to send soldiers to Charleston Harbor. When Lincoln first suggested war, Montgomery Blair was the only member of the cabinet who agreed.

Blair's father had already demanded it of Lincoln. Like Lincoln, Blair knew that an independent South would kill the party and his family ambitions. The Blairs did not hate the South; they just liked themselves. That tells what kind of principle those men had. It tells exactly what the war was all about.

The deepest injury ever inflicted on the people of the united States was the war Abraham Lincoln made to prevent Southern Independence. That war brought to Americans more destruction, suffering, death than all their other wars combined. It wreaked severe ecological disaster. Claimed after the fact to have been fought on the black people's behalf, it caused during or from its effects the death of an estimated fourth of their number. It blighted the land and impoverished a good part of the people for four score years.

That was the injury to the South. To the North it made a society called "Gilded"– shining on outside, rotten within.

To all sections of the country it brought an injury not physical, but deeper and never healing. The war made a revolution that changed the form of government of the United States. It extinguished a republic and set in its place the empire. From thence came socialism, the all-powerful government, loss of freedom.

There was a time when people had to fear personal attack from only nearby sources—nature or a nearby individual; they did not have to fear their distant sovereign. Samuel Johnson (1709-1784) lived in and described such a happy time: royalty lacked both desire and power to do the people much harm. Personal misery came from individual causes, not from government. That interval ended in 1861: a president made a war, then using the power of war office, made a revolution that transformed the government he commanded. All Lincoln had to do to avoid the horrors of war was just not make one.

Abraham Lincoln's deed was a true cataclysm, it made a new country and hastened a new epoch in history. He changed forever the relationship between government and citizen. Lincoln weakened the citizen and empowered the ruler. Life and death have never been the same since. Rulers thenceforth gained power over life and death. They have wielded that power. Since Lincoln, most of the misery to which Americans are subject is inflicted on them by their own officers, to whom they are indeed subjects.

The Southern Independence War was a bad one. The effects of the Southern Independence War were not confined to one place, they radiated centrifugally over the world, setting in motion forces leading to later horrors—mega-governments and mega-wars, rise of socialism and its child Communism, perpetual war "for perpetual peace," replacement of God by government, social disorder, class hate, loss of freedom, moral blight, growing race disharmony.

Abraham Lincoln started a war to prevent Southern independence. It did not take a genius to conceive it. His Mexican War embarrassment had taught him that once a war is in motion it is hard to stop. The "Star of the West" had taught him how to start it. The state of South Carolina had fired a warning shot at that ship bringing troops to Fort Sumter, three months earlier. The ship turned away. President Buchanan made nothing of it and neither did the American people. Lincoln's scheme was to devise a "Spot" and a "Shot" which he could use to start a war and blame it on the South. The South, knowing their fate was in his hands, waited in dread.

As soon as he was inaugurated Lincoln went immediately to work to make a war. He deliberately planned his stratagem. He executed a classical conspiracy.

Throughout his career, in accord with his scheming nature, Lincoln would advise his party fellows: "Be ever so quiet, that the enemy shall not be informed." He practiced that tactic even within his party, against rivals. To him, everything was politics. He had no other life, no other conception of life. During the war he saw no difference between the Confederate Army and his critics in the

North. They both threatened his position. Secretly, the plot went forward.

It is one thing to want war. It is another thing to commit it. It was a sin for the money men to urge Lincoln to war. It is wrong to want murder, but to think it does less harm than to do it. The desire was the Republican Party's but the act was Abraham Lincoln's. He could have thought of the destruction, injury, suffering, death that would be necessary for his party to prevail, of the cost in blood to his countrymen.

"Politics is self-interest pretending to principle." Lincoln's party, pursuing power, pretended principle—"slavery." That sham gave them power. "Government is the conduct of public affairs for private interest." The Republicans started a war to hold and extend their interests in place and plunder. They sacrificed the American people by the most horrible of human acts—war. That is why government must be kept small, its powers limited, its officers restrained.

A Dirty Piece of Work: The Invasion of Charleston Harbor

ON MARCH 4, 1861, ABRAHAM LINCOLN was inaugurated as president. Now possessing the power he immediately began making plans to use it for his party. Rulers make war on weaker neighbors; the classical strategy is to blame the other side for starting it as the Nazis did in World War II. Charleston Harbor presented an obvious way to accomplish that aim. Quiet preparations began.

Fort Sumter was of no possible use to anyone except a power desiring to capture South Carolina by force of arms. South Carolina, a sovereign state, had joined a union voluntarily. Not a single person had suggested that membership was compulsory. South Carolina had withdrawn from the union three months before Lincoln was inaugurated. The country was unharmed. South Carolina was no threat to the states remaining in the Union. Whether that state was in or out would not hurt a single person still in the Union. The purpose of Fort Sumter was to protect Charleston and South Carolina. South Carolina and the Confederacy had offered to pay for U.S. property in the seceded states, to take their share of the national debt, and to discuss any necessary adjustments. South Carolina committed no act of aggression.

A large group of people instinctively felt that war, the worst of all horrors, was unthinkable.

Commander-in-Chief Winfield Scott wanted to evacuate the fort. What good would it do to make war? What good would it do to devastate the land? Say to the seceded states, "Wayward sisters, depart in peace." Lincoln told Scott that he would order Fort

Sumter peacefully evacuated. That intention was passed to the fort commander, Major Robert Anderson.

11 MARCH: Lincoln has Scott write an order to Major Anderson to evacuate the Fort but tells Scott not to send it until further instructions. When did Lincoln decide on war? It was on 11 March that the Confederate Congress enacted the low tariff that so inflamed Lincoln's party. Anderson will not be told the truth until April 8th or 9th, when Federal warships arrive at Charleston Harbor.

Senator Douglas wanted peace, tried to use his influence to that end, and was led to believe that Lincoln would maintain peace. Senator James M. Mason of Virginia, descendant of the esteemed George Mason whose ideas contributed toward Declaration of Independence and Constitution, knew better. "The only way to maintain peace is to withdraw troops from the seceded states. If Lincoln uses force, Virginia and other states will secede. John Bell, recent candidate for president, warned Lincoln that if he used force more states would secede, that he should keep the peace, not invade.

Even Senator Seward, now Secretary of State, wanted peace, advised against invading.

The Confederate Government sent three commissioners to Washington to negotiate resolution of differences. Lincoln refused to talk to them although Seward did unofficially through a third party. As he was in all intercourse, even personal, Lincoln remained impenetrable, vague.

The Northern people, of both parties, the newspapers, expected that Fort Sumter would be evacuated, peace maintained, and the nation the better for it. There was no clamor for war. Many Republican politicians acquiesced in peace. The country seemed to be accepting the Confederacy as no threat to anybody's happiness.

But it was a threat to the happiness of the party possessing control of the Federal executive branch.

The obvious way to bring on a war and blame the South was at Charleston. It did not take a genius to know it. It was openly discussed. Fort Sumter was the key to control of the harbor and its custom duties. South Carolina would want it to protect its territory, the Republicans would want it to protect their tariff. South Carolina was out of the Union but the Federal Government had soldiers on Fort Sumter. The question was: how to make South Carolina fire at the fort? That was easy, too. The Confederacy had already made it clear that Charleston Harbor was for South Carolina, that Fort Sumter was for the defense of South Carolina, the Federal Government had no need for it now. They had made that point clear by firing a warning shot at a United States vessel three months ago.

The first act of aggression was the Federal army taking possession of the deserted little islet. They had no legitimate business there. That hostile act alarmed South Carolina, but they did not respond, rather continued supplying the soldiers daily with fresh produce from the Charleston market two miles away.

The power-seeking Blair family of Maryland and Missouri wanted war. There were four of them: the father, Francis P.; son Montgomery, postmaster general in Lincoln's cabinet; son Frank, Congressman and soon to be a general; and son-in-law, Gustavus Vasa Fox, assistant secretary of Navy. The Blairs, said to have a shortage of intelligence but a surplus of ambition, were former Democrats, one of those families always prominent because they pursue prominence, rush to the centers of power, regardless of party or principle. Like Lincoln, they were "trimmers." Like Lincoln, Blair wanted to send the black people to Africa. But, he wanted even more to grasp power. The Blairs and Lincoln were going to become powerful by war.

---

15 MARCH: Lincoln asked his cabinet members to each give him a written opinion on invading Charleston Harbor, what he called, in his usual dissembling way, "to provision Fort Sumter." Seward, Chase, Welles, Bates, and Cameron opposed it. They considered war in a way Lincoln never did, that war is of itself worse than the alternative. Even if for policy rather than moral, it is to their credit that their first instinct was to oppose the horror of war. Montgomery Blair was the only cabinet member who

urged war. His father, Francis, or Frank, heatedly told Lincoln he would be a coward if he did not invade. The Blairs asserted that going into Charleston Harbor would cause no war.

Also on March 15 in the Senate, Douglas attacked the Blairs. He told the truth:

> "What they really want is a civil war. They are determined, first, on seeing slavery abolished by force, and then on expelling the entire Negro race from the continent. This was old Blair's doctrine, Sir, long ago, and it is Montgomery's doctrine, Sir. If they can get and keep their grip on Lincoln, this country will never see peace or prosperity again, Sir, in your time or mine, or in our children's time.
>
> The president of the United States holds the destiny of this country in his hands. I believe he means peace, and war will be averted, unless he is over ruled by the disunion faction of his party. We all know the irrepressible conflict is going on in his camp, even debating whether Fort Sumter shall be surrendered when it is impossible to hold it; whether Major Anderson shall not be kept there until he starves to death, or applies the torch with his own hand to the match that blows him and his little garrison into eternity, for fear that somebody in the Republican party might say you had backed down.
>
> What man in all America, who knows the facts connected with Fort Sumter, can hesitate in saying that duty, honor, patriotism and humanity require that Anderson and his gallant band should be instantly withdrawn? Sir, I am not afraid to say so. I would scorn to take party advantage or manufacture partisan capital out of an act of patriotism. Throw aside this party squabble about how you are going to get along with your party pledges before the election. Peace is the only policy that can save the country and save your party."

Douglas said he would not let the "war wing" Republicans prevail. "I know their scheme. I do not mean to let them plunge this country into war." Douglas must be given credit for fighting for peace. Just as before the election he accurately predicted the damage Lincoln would do, he again predicted the truth. He spoke of the "War Wing" of the Republican Party. They did what he said they would. Lincoln did what they told him to do.

19 MARCH: Senator Thomas Clingman of North Carolina said Lincoln would not call Congress into session because, if he would ask them to go to war against the Confederate states, "I do not believe they would agree to do it." He made this perfect prophecy: "The Republicans intend ... as soon as they can collect the force to have a war, to begin; and then call Congress suddenly together and say, 'The honor of the country is concerned; the flag is insulted. You must come up and vote men and money.'" That is exactly what did occur.

While the public dreaded the horror of war, the ruling party dreaded the horror of peace. The party elite cared more for their power than for their people. Anybody who doubts that the power drive is the strongest and wickedest of the sins need look no farther than the Blair family and Lincoln.

In their safe haven they plotted danger for everybody else. The Blairs' in-law, Gustavus Vasa Fox, suggested an expedition into Charleston Harbor. Carrying ostensibly food, and below decks an army, to land at Sumter, and either discredit the Confederates by landing unopposed, or preferably provoking a defensive shot which Lincoln could exploit to start war. To make matters certain Fox asked Lincoln to send him to Charleston to visit the fort and learn the circumstances there. South Carolina Governor Pickens, like all the Confederates, straining to avoid war, gave permission on Fox's pledge that he was there only for peaceful purposes.

21 MARCH: Fox interviews Governor Pickens and is allowed to visit Major Anderson. The information he got showed them how to organize their conspiracy. Lincoln's next spy was Ward Hill Lamon, Lincoln's young law partner and bodyguard. Lamon told Governor Pickens he had come to Charleston as Lincoln's agent to arrange removal of the garrison from Fort Sumter. He asked if a warship could come into Charleston Harbor to remove the troops. Pickens told him that no war vessel would be allowed, only an ordinary ship. Lamon visited Anderson for a private interview, returned to the governor and said he would be back in a few days to arrange evacuation. He never came back to Charleston.

Lincoln then knew for certain what was known anyhow: Charleston would not permit war ships in their harbor. He learned it in a dishonorable way.

28 MARCH: Lincoln read to his cabinet a letter from General Scott, strongly urging him to give up Fort Pickens and Fort Sumter because peace was infinitely better than war. Postmaster General Montgomery Blair threatened to resign if Lincoln did not invade. Blair would never have resigned, but he knew Lincoln. Scott, the real warrior, a man who had proved his bravery, wanted peace; Blair, the politician whose only credential was greed, demanded war.

29 MARCH: The cabinet met again. Opposition to war began to weaken. Republican Party pressure was affecting them. Seward, however, still stood for peace: "The dispatch of an expedition to Fort Sumter would provoke attack and involve war. I would instruct Major Anderson to retire from Sumter, forthwith." Seward and Scott desired peace. They could not escape their naive belief that peace was better than war.

Lincoln ordered Fox to invade Charleston Harbor. He would call it a peaceful mission, not "aggression," not "invasion." If the ships should be attacked he would blame the Confederates for firing the first shot and get an excuse to start war. Lincoln wrote Secretary of War Cameron, "I desire that an expedition to move by sea, be got ready to sail as early as the 6th of April."

While many Republicans recoiled at the horror of war, there is no evidence that Lincoln gave it a thought, then or ever. It was just another exercise in party strategy to him. Lincoln, the chief politician, was aware only of party welfare. The party needed war. They gain power by war, lose existence by peace. They wanted control of the Federal Government; they wanted government to execute their financial policy, a tariff to subsidize their mills, and "internal improvements" to subsidize their business. But there were still many merchants and financiers of the Eastern cities who wanted peace.

30 MARCH: Governor Pickens wired the three Confederate commissioners in Washington to ask why the garrison remained

at Fort Sumter long after Lamon had positively assured him it would leave, fifteen days after Seward had given his pledge that the fort would be quickly evacuated.

4 APRIL: John B. Baldwin, a Virginia pro-Union leader, tells Lincoln that if he will withdraw troops from Sumter and Pickens Virginia would not secede, peace would endure. Lincoln assured Baldwin, as he had been saying publicly, that he wanted peace. But, on the same day a group of Republican governors demanded that he make war, that they will give him money and men. He agreed with them. Lincoln said one thing to one group, the very opposite to another, both statements couched in vague terms, safe for him.

He was famous for that method back in Illinois.

6 APRIL: Lincoln wrote a terse statement: "I am directed by the President of the United States to notify you to expect an attempt will be made to supply Fort Sumter with provisions only, and that, if such an attempt be not resisted, no effort to throw in men, arms, or ammunition will be made without further notice, or in case of an attack upon the fort." He called to his office Robert S. Chew, a minor official in State Department, told him to go to Governor Pickens, read the statement, hand it to him, say nothing else, and leave.

7 APRIL: Lincoln told Virginian John Minor Botts, a fellow Whig whom he knew in Congress in 1848, that he wanted peace and to assure the South. He then ordered Northern governors to mobilize their militia.

8 APRIL: Lincoln's messenger, Robert Chew, traveled to Charleston, met Governor Pickens and General Beauregard, read the declaration, handed it to Pickens, declined to accept an answer, and promptly departed. To that insult, Lincoln would later add injury. Governor Pickens is to witness his daughter, during her wedding ceremony, shot dead by Lincoln's guns.

8 OR 9 APRIL: Major Anderson received a letter from the Federal War Department. He is astonished. He had been told that he would be ordered to evacuate the fort without a fight, but was

now told that he was to hold on at all costs until relieved by an invading fleet. Anderson has been purposely deceived. He wrote, "We shall strive to do our duty, though I frankly say that my heart is not in the war which I see is to be thus commenced. That God will still avert it, and cause us to resort to pacific measures to maintain our rights, is my ardent prayer." Anderson proved Lincoln started the war.

9 APRIL: Lincoln's fleet arrived at Charleston. The city is shocked to see six warships off the bar. Governor Pickens realized he was a victim of treachery. He had permitted Fox and Lamon to visit the fort after they had promised that mission was strictly "pacific, to arrange evacuation." One might say the war started that day. Lincoln's force arrived off the harbor on that date, but the South did not fire. The startled Southerners, knowing they had been deceived and betrayed, suffered three days of indecision. Lincoln had lied to them, what was he going to do next? Would he come on and land in the town, itself? They knew they could better protect themselves before the fleet landed soldiers.

On April 9 also Lincoln, his wife, and a party, rode out to Oak Hill Cemetery. Lincoln tells reporters, "The country will see whether they dare fire upon an unarmed vessel carrying relief to our starving soldiers." An accompanying reporter wrote: "He expressed little hope for peace, intimated a determination to relieve Major Anderson and hold other Southern forts at all hazards." Lincoln was in a cheerful mood.

10 APRIL: Ex-Senator Wigfall telegraphed from Charleston to President Davis in Montgomery: "Lincoln intends war. Delay is to his advantage and our disadvantage. Let us take Fort Sumter before we have to fight the fleet and the fort."

11 APRIL: Confederate commissioners in Washington sent their last dispatch: "... the main object of the expedition is the relief of Sumter ... a force will be landed which will overcome all opposition." To Seward the chairman of the Confederate commission wrote a letter:

> "We must go home and tell our countrymen that our earnest and ceaseless efforts in behalf of peace have been futile, that

the government of the United States means to subjugate them by force of arms. Impartial history will record the innocence of the Confederacy and blame the federal government for the blood and mourning that will result from the war. The military demonstration against the people of the seceded states are inconsistent with Seward's own theory that these states are still component parts of the late American Union, that there is no Constitutional power in the president of the United States to levy war without the consent of Congress, against a foreign people, much less against any portion of the people of the United States. We have been abused and overreached. The leaders of the government at Montgomery will believe that there has been a systematic duplicity practiced on them through me."

Seward never replied to the letter. President Davis told the Confederate Congress, "The crooked paths of diplomacy can scarcely furnish an example so wanting in courtesy, in candor and directness, as was the course of the United States Government toward our commissioners in Washington." The Lincoln administration "followed a protracted course of fraud and prevarication. Every pledge made was broken, and every assurance of good faith was followed by an act of perfidy."

The Democratic *New York Herald* said Lincoln had made a fatal mistake in sending the fleet to Charleston and thus provoking civil war. "Our only hope now against civil war of indefinite duration seems to lie in the overthrow of the demoralizing, disorganizing and destructive sectional party of which 'Honest Abe' Lincoln is the pliant instrument." A good part of the American people were going to be hurt worse by a man they had never seen than by anybody they had ever known.

12 APRIL: The Confederacy sent off the first shell toward Sumter at 4:30 a.m., Friday, April 12, 1861. When the news was flashed to Washington, Lincoln exultantly declared, "I knew they would do it!" His anxiety was relieved. That of his countrymen was just beginning. Lincoln would soak the South with his countrymen's blood. One single selfish man would have on his hands the blood of a million. Lincoln did not mind the stain or the

soaking, and has never been called to account for it. He is worshiped for it. His flotilla, invading Charleston arbor, inciting the Confederacy to fire, gave him excuse to start war and blame the other side. The Confederacy's bloodless cannonade was merely response to aggression. They knew the political risks of firing and the military risk of not firing. They did not know to what lengths the Republicans would go. They concluded that self-protection gave them no alternative but to prevent the landing.

13 APRIL: Major Anderson surrendered the fort.

SUNDAY, 14 APRIL: Abraham Lincoln decided to make war on his own people. The most momentous day in the life of Abraham Lincoln. It is to that day that he owes his renown. That day delivered Lincoln from the obscurity he hated into the kingdom and the power and the glory he spent his life seeking. He had finally reached his goal—secular immortality. The only kind he believed in. If Lincoln could have mustered Christian humility enough to resist the Devil's Proposition, he would have denied himself, and served his neighbor. And saved his country. But, he would have died unknown. Like the better men Millard Fillmore, Franklin Pierce, and James Buchanan. April 14, 1861, was also the most fateful day in the life of America. Lincoln seized the moment. "They have fired on 'Old Glory.' We are at war!" He "declared" war by himself. The Constitution gives war-making power to Congress only. The Constitution provides that Federal forces can enter a state only at the invitation of its governor or legislature. He contradicted his own pronouncement in 1848 that all people have a right to self-government. Lincoln declared war on the South. He called up an army, ordered a levy of troops from each state, and embarked upon military despotism. He did not declare war, he merely made war. He did not have to go to war. All he had to do to avoid a war was simply not start one. But, he was aching to start one, had been willing for years, considering it since November, and conspiring it for a month.

Many people believe there would have been no war if any of the candidates other than Lincoln had become president of the United States.

The same speculation can apply to the other side. Robert Toombs, former Senator from Georgia was now Confederate secretary of State. He was effective, popular, assertive, a good thinker and speaker. He had been an early and vigorous advocate of the need to secede from an oppressive government. There was strong support to elect him president of the Confederate States, many people thought Davis honest and able, but rigid, lacking the understanding of people that Toombs had, that Tombs had more insight, would make a better leader. Davis did not want the presidency, took it as duty. If he had declined, or if Toombs had been elected, history might have been different.

Toombs opposed firing on the fort. He said Lincoln invaded for the purpose of starting war, and would use firing on the fort to bring the Northern people in on his side. "This puts us in the wrong. It would be suicide, murder, will lose us every friend in the North. It will inaugurate a civil war greater than any the world has yet seen." If Toombs had been president there would have been no firing on Fort Sumter, Lincoln would have had a more difficult task engineering a war, and, in retrospect, without war, the Confederacy would have succeeded. History would have written a different story. A dream much to be desired.

South Carolina had warned off the "Star of the West" from landing at Fort Sumter. Why did not the North then rise up in wrath and fly to arms? President Buchanan chose to ignore it. So did the American people. It took a second shot, skillfully triggered by Lincoln. Firing on the "Star of the West" demonstrated that the South would protect its harbor, its port, its land. All one had to do to start a war was to make them fire again, only this time make a war, and blame it on them.

That Lincoln deliberately started war is proven by ample evidence. Not only the facts of the event itself, but by testimony. Captain Gustavus Fox, Blair in-law, was author of the Charleston Harbor conspiracy. Lincoln wrote him congratulations on the success of their project, telling Fox that they accomplished more by the expedition being turned back than if they had landed. Thus, he himself acknowledged his scheme.

In July, 1861, newly-appointed Illinois Senator Orville Browning arrived in Washington. The first thing he did was go immediately that night to see Lincoln. Browning had taken the seat held by Stephen Douglas. He had replaced the man who had been Lincoln's nemesis, the man who was a lifelong goad to the envy of the power-fixed Lincoln, the man who had exceeded Lincoln all his life, until the last contest. Douglas was not only defeated for president but had suffered the ultimate defeat—death. Lincoln was now relieved of the prominent rival and now supplied with a Republican one. Browning was a political ally and social friend of Lincoln for twenty-five years. Lincoln had once written Mrs. Browning a long, cynical letter, ridiculing in the unkindest terms a woman Lincoln discarded.

Now, Lincoln president, Browning senator, they sat in the high seat, savoring their rise. Lincoln was glad to see his crony. The most close-mouthed and reticent of the politicians, yet he could not forbear boasting of his achievement. By this time his party war was made, accepted by the Northern people, now humming along. Lincoln knew Browning was safe. For once, he let down his guard. He had to tell somebody of his success, the exhilarating access of power that he, singlehanded, had brought about by his shrewd piece of political work. The party was now safe, and he had done it all. He told in detail the story of his intrigue to Browning, who went home and that night before going to bed and wrote it in his secret diary. It remained secret for four score years.

There are other witnesses. James Harvey, a Philadelphia reporter, a Republican and acquaintance of William Seward, learned of Lincoln's plan to deceive the Southerners and elicit a military response before it was executed. He sent a series of warning telegrams to prominent South Carolinian Andrew Magrath, a boyhood friend. After the war Harvey was appointed to an ambassadorship. Radical Republicans discovered his old telegrams and raised a furor to remove him from office on the grounds of party disloyalty.

Congressman Alexander Long, a Democrat from Ohio, in a speech to the House of Representatives on April 8, 1864. He said he was present when Lincoln was told that Fort Sumter had been fired on. When he heard the news Lincoln was exultant, exclaiming, "I knew they would do it!" Republicans tried to expel Long from Congress for telling the truth but could not quite muster a two-thirds majority.

Lincoln started a war. To be sure to act without hindrance he refused to call Congress into session. By the time they met he had perhaps 300,000 men under arms. The War to Prevent Southern Independence did not begin with the firing on Fort Sumter; it began with an invasion of the port of Charleston. To say that the war began with the firing on Fort Sumter is like saying the war with Japan began with shooting at the Japanese airplanes at Pearl Harbor.

The "slavery issue" was a tool to gain office. "Fort Sumter" was a tool to hold it. The attack on Charleston Harbor, miscalled Fort Sumter, was Abraham Lincoln's declaration of war.

Two Wars

"We protest against our legal withdrawal from the union being called rebellion. We protest against having our children and grandchildren taught from histories written by our military antagonists, by our sectional and political enemies. Our descendants are being taught that their forefathers were rebels and traitors, when our national capitol bears the name and perpetuates the fame of the secessionist, rebel, and traitor, George Washington."

—COLONEL ROBERT BINGHAM, CONFEDERATE VETERAN AND NOTED EDUCATOR, ADDRESS AT THE 50TH ANNIVERSARY OF HIS GRADUATION FROM THE UNIVERSITY OF NORTH CAROLINA, JUNE 3, 1905.

"The great debt that capitalists will see to it is made out of the war must be used as a means to control the volume of money."

—WALL STREET PRIVATE CIRCULAR, 1861

THE WAR TO PREVENT SOUTHERN Independence was two different wars: one in the North, quite another in the South. European visitors to America during the war reported that in the South the war's damaging effects could be seen everywhere, its devastation could not be escaped. "In the North," observed a British visitor, "You would not know there was a war going on unless you went to Washington City."

Colonel Fremantle, the widely-traveled British military observer, wrote shortly after the battle of Gettysburg: "Luxury and comfort strike one as extraordinary. The streets are full of well-dressed people, crowded with able-bodied citizens, capable of bearing arms, with no intention of doing so. Bounties [for enlistment] of $550 are offered. They don't feel the war at all here. Unless there is a smash of their money, or some other catastrophe, they won't feel the war, will have no desire to make peace."

In June 1863, William Oates led his Alabama regiment into southern Pennsylvania. Theirs was a restrained incursion. They warred on no civilians, they preyed on nobody. It may not have been peaceable, but it was peaceful. They were astonished to see a land so healthy and unravaged. That is not all that astonished them. The Alabamians had opportunity to talk at length with the people along the way. They spent awhile with people of substance. Colonel Oates and his men were shocked at the lack of involvement of the Northern people. The war had ignored them. And they had ignored the war. They were indifferent toward it, saw Lincoln only as an ambitious man who had made his way to high place. Colonel Oates wrote of his experiences:

> "Even among the better-educated class of society in the North, the war, overwhelming in the South, was only a distant event, of which they had no knowledge. It did not touch them. They were aware of, but indifferent to, national politics. These people, apparently well-informed on general subjects of culture, were remarkably ignorant of the causes of the war, and the real character of the Confederate Government. They looked upon the war as a personal contention between two ambitious men for supremacy; they seemed to think that President Davis wanted to leave the union merely to become president of the Southern Confederacy. One of the ladies said she wished that the two armies would hang the two presidents, Jefferson Davis and Lincoln, and stop the war."

Lincoln was never secure in office. His party lost in 1862, and in 1864 the vote against him increased by 10%. That occurred despite enormous advantages: power of office and patronage, arrest of political opponents, 35,000 anti-Lincoln voters in jail, suppression of hundreds of newspapers, bayonet-point counting the votes in New York City and in many states, the hasty admission of new and favorable state governments, and management of the soldier vote. Despite military force in New York City, Lincoln got less than half the vote. He carried New York State by 50.47%. If the Democrats had nominated Horatio Seymour Lincoln might have lost, the war would have been stopped, and two-thirds of the deaths would have been prevented. He lost Kentucky and Delaware despite military occupation. He won 2.2 million votes or 55% out of a 4 million total. He carried the three biggest states—New York, Pennsylvania, and Ohio by only 86,000 votes—930,000 to 844,000. If those three states, won so narrowly, had gone to McClellan, and two or three states had joined them, Lincoln would have lost.

In Illinois, Lincoln lost his own county, Sangamon, and all bounding counties. The soldier vote, manipulated and managed on his behalf, counted by his agents, made his victory. In all wars soldiers vote for their commander. Poor wretches, they must justify their sacrifice. "The people look upon those set in authority over them as benefactors." They esteem their commander because he commands.

His soldiers never learned it, but Lincoln did them no good. They gave him their votes and their lives, he took their votes and their lives. Lincoln came to high place not as benefactor but as malefactor—the lifelong pursuit of worldly power, the Devil's Proposition. A few people knew it. Lincoln did not rise by winning the votes of acquaintances, but of strangers. Matheny, best man in Lincoln's wedding, and Dubois, a neighbor a few houses down, said Lincoln was insincere and "not always honest." Herndon said more than once that Lincoln's peers in the county did not like him.

Recruitment was the Federal Government's chief problem. Would that the Confederacy were so lucky. The Republican administration during the war spent one-fourth of the total federal budget on recruitment. That program, they admitted, was a failure. Northern boys did not rush to join Lincoln's army. Harvard had exactly half as many of its alumni to die in the Confederate Army as in the Federal Army—64 to128, but the Harvard student body was never half Southern. (Even today Harvard honors its German Nazi and Japanese alumni but not its Confederate.)

The facts deny Northern passion for their war. The newspapers called it "patriotic" when a family would save their son by paying the fee to buy a substitute from the destitute. The Abolitionists' sons found urgent business calling them to Europe for the duration. Let a modern American look to see how many of the intellectuals of Boston got in the war. Whenever a man of that period is mentioned in present day writing, one can look to see if he was in the war. Usually not. To carry on their war the Republicans recruited the Blacks, mainly by force and bribery. Black troops were held in contempt and used mostly as labor, in forlorn hopes, and as officers' servants and concubines. Every seized South Carolina slave in a "Massachusetts" regiment was another New Englander who could stay home.

THE GREAT EMANCIPATOR

Blacks were in the war so that the Abolitionists could evade it. Blacks were invited because whites declined the invitation. Orders that may be seen many times in the Official Records were to recruit blacks by money; if that failed, take them by force into the army.

There was no cry among the Negroes for freedom. The "issue" did not come from them. It was entirely a political campaign. The hypocrisy of Lincoln's reputation as morally opposed to slavery is shown by his declaration to exclude Negroes from voting or holding office. Lincoln's career positions on slavery, the Negro, or any issue, are so various that the only explanation for them is political.

The state of Illinois voted in 1862 to prohibit Negro and mulatto migration into that state. The issue was merely political, totally for the benefit of a political party. What the anti-Democrats politicians did with that issue in 1854 and thereafter, was treason.

Herein was the treason: Slavery, the institution, was irrelevant to the quarrel. "Slavery," the "issue" was a dishonest weapon of political war. The agitation of "slavery" was selfish and destructive. The agitators had made the "slavery issue." They debased a question that should have been allowed gradual settling as it did in the rest of the Americas.

The Abolitionists themselves were hypocrites, radicals, acting not from love of the black, but hatred of the white, seizing on slavery to strengthen their unpopular with a subject abstractly appealing to everybody. Lincoln's party cynically combined slavery with Northern desire to exclude Negro migration, scared them with a phantom threat, and called it "anti-slavery." It was not anti-slavery, it was anti-Negro. He had divided his country. That was Lincoln's peace-time treason, his second-worst crime.

Lincoln made war for his party. The "slaves" were merely servants to serve his party. So were the soldiers in his war. He killed them both. His war was a projection of his politics. "Slavery," then "Union,"—each only a tool to be put to the use of his party.

"Slavery" was a tool to win election, discarded once elected. "Union" took its place as a tool to justify war. That tool lost its edge in 1862. Robert E. Lee was winning battles, the Republicans losing them, not just military, but against the real enemy, the Democrats, in November elections. They were losing the battle for public support, both Northern and European, losing recruitment, losing Boston boys flying from the war, urgent business calling them to foreign climes, and faced with a strong and growing peace movement.

The Republicans were worried. In December, battle humiliations at Fredericksburg and at White Hall, North Carolina, raised worry to panic. The atrocities in the latter place, December 16-17, 1862, were covered up and are little known. A federal force of 30,000 left occupied Goldsboro with the intention of cutting the vital Wilmington & Weldon Railroad and destroying the Confederate ironclad *Neuse* under construction on the river. The Union force was repulsed by 200 Confederate home guards, including several black men. The Yankees were unable to cross the bridge. In retaliation they bombarded and burned the village of White Hall with numerous civilian casualties.

In Springfield Lincoln was known as "lazy," and "spoiled his children." But, on Christmas Eve, he went to work, and forgot his children. By that night he had induced the passive Burnside to take Lincoln's blame for Fredericksburg and promoted five generals for failing but agreeing to hide the fight at White Hall. Lincoln and the money party elite looked defeat in the face.

Lincoln described the situation:

"Things had gone from bad to worse, we had reached the end of our rope, we had about played our last card. We must change tactics or lose the game. I determined to adopt the Emancipation policy."

He, even the Abolitionists, admitted it was illegal, a "war" measure, to foment revolution behind enemy lines and to give a cause to the Republican Party war of usurpation. It had two aims: political—to prevent foreign nations from recognizing the Confederacy and to give the indifferent North a reason to support his flagging war; and military. The political aim succeeded—"slavery" was grafted onto his party, slavery gilded the gold party. The Republicans had a "cause"; they could claim to be making war for "freedom." The Military aim failed—the slaves rose up nowhere. The truth is, black and white were more loyal in the beleaguered South than the whites were in the war-prospering North.

The great Emancipator was not Abraham Lincoln, it was John Murray, Lord Dunmore, last Colonial Governor of Virginia, who freed the slaves first—in 1775. Only his proclamation did not stick—he lost his war. Or was the Great Emancipator Lord Berkeley, Colonial Governor, who did it in 1676; or Nathaniel Bacon, his enemy, who also did it? For the same reason all of them—a war measure. Lincoln admitted his was a war measure, forced by failure ("We'd about played our last card"). Since the beginning of warfare invaders have freed slaves to gain adherents and foment insurrection. The Republicans sent into the South agents, propaganda, and money urging slaves to revolt. The only worry Lincoln ever expressed about it was: "When the Negroes rise up, and begin violence it will play havoc with public opinion in the North and in Europe." There was no violence, except his. The Negroes of the South mostly remained quiet.

Lincoln's statement proves his vicious motive, demonstrates his cold-blooded indifference to anticipated suffering, reveals his ignorance of the true relationship, the close bond, between the two races in the South. George Christian, of Richmond said it well:

"If the system of labor on the Southern farms was so cruel and barbarous, if the Negroes were slave objects, and not servants trusted and well cared for, why was it that when the Southern homes were stripped of their defenders off in the Confederate armies, why then did not the Negroes, conscious of their power, rape, and kill, and burn? By so doing, they could have in forty-eight hours, broken up the Confederate armies defending the South, whose soldiers would have rushed back home to protect their families ... The fact is, the Negroes, conscious of their power, were equally conscious of their responsibility, were more loyal, and tenderly dutiful than at any time in their history. The truth is, the institution of slavery had knit the hearts of the races together too tenderly to suggest such an extreme event to either race."

Lincoln's act of "emancipation" demonstrates how some people are willing to inflict great injury for small profit. Burn a village to cook supper. Lincoln destroyed that part of the union that supported the black people. A peaceful evolution would have provided for them. But as a result of his war and his policy, the slaves, formerly cared for, were turned out into harsh conditions. They suffered extreme material and physical injury. A fourth of the Negro population died as a result of Lincoln's war. He killed a million people including civilians. He made half his country a wasteland. White and black suffered and died together. Sherman's Georgia/South Carolina campaign alone has been described by *Smithsonian* magazine as the fourth-worst American ecological disaster. Southern injury took four-score years to repair.

Lincoln dishonestly used "slavery" to create disunion, revealing he did not love the union; he dishonestly used "Union" to make a slave-injuring war, revealing that he did not love the slave. The slaves were hurt immediately by privation, wounds, epidemics, personal attack, forced from their homes, declared contraband, forced into service of Lincoln's army. Sherman's army—not only his—did more insult to colored than to white. They took the watches, valuables, of every colored person on the Andrews farm. "Mama" Betsy Palmer said, "I have knowed white folks all my life, some sorry ones, some mean ones. Yankees is de fust ever I seed mean enough to steal from Niggers." (Accent, grammar, words, are old English. Both races talked that way. Some still do. It is old, not wrong.)

Raphael Semmes was a very articulate and insightful man who was to become the Confederacy's greatest naval hero. On August 5, 1861, his Confederate ship was anchored at Port of Spain, Trinidad, then a British colony. Her commander, Semmes, was entertaining Captain Hillyar of a nearby British ship. Semmes told Hillyar that the war would be long and bloody. Asked about the cause of the war, Semmes told the Englishman:

> "Our late co-partners [the North] did not treat us in an honest manner; we are defending ourselves against robbers, with knives at our throats. The machinery of the Federal Government, under which we have lived, and which was designed for the common benefit, had been made the means of despoiling the South, to enrich the North. The iniquitous tariffs, under the operation of which the South had in effect been reduced to a dependent colonial condition, almost as abject as that of the Roman provinces, the only difference being that smooth-faced hypocrisy had been added to robbery, inasmuch as we had been plundered under the forms of law."

Captain Hillyar replied, "All of this is new to me, I assure you. I thought that your war had risen out of the slavery question." Semmes answered:

> "That is a common mistake of foreigners. The enemy has taken pains to impress foreign nations with this false view of the case. With the exception of a few sincere zealots the canting, hypocritical Yankee cares as little for our slaves as he does for our draft animals. The war which he has been making upon slavery for the last forty years is only a by-play a device to help on his main action—Empire. It is a curious coincidence that the slavery agitation only commenced at the time that the North

began to rob the South by its tariffs. The slavery question was no more than an implement employed by a robber to rob the South. It strengthened the Northern party, and enabled them to get their tariffs through Congress. When at length the South, driven to the wall, turned, as even the crushed worm will turn, and seceded, the North made war to prevent our leaving. They cunningly perceived that "No Slavery" would be a popular war-cry, and they gave that as a cause for war. It is true, we are defending our slave property, but we are defending it no more than we are defending any species of our property. What, in fact, we are doing, is fighting for our independence. Our forefathers made a great mistake when they warmed the Puritan serpent to their bosom. We, their descendants, are endeavoring to remedy that mistake.

Summary

"Ambition has its reward in the pride, pomp, and circumstances of glorious war."

—RANDOLPH OF ROANOKE

"Of historical characters, Lincoln is most like Lenin."

—EDMUND WILSON

"No single man makes history. But revolutions are made by men of action with one-track minds, geniuses in their ability to confine themselves to a limited field. They overturn the old order in a few hours or days, the whole upheaval takes only a few weeks or years. But the evil spirit that inspired the upheavals is worshiped for decades thereafter, for centuries."

—BORIS PASTERNAK.

ABRAHAM LINCOLN MADE A WAR to prevent Southern independence. Why did he do it?

The young Abraham Lincoln, chided for insolent behavior, was asked, "Abe, if you keep on like this, where in the world are you going to end up?" "President of the United States," he coolly answered. The boy often predicted that end, not as a wish but as his practical intent. No other future American president had the plan so young, revealed it so plain, or pursued it so exclusively. His run was relentless. From early childhood he was a politician, a showman, a public entertainer. He was not a deep thinker, a candid speaker, or a moral superior. He had one interest: political ambition.

At the age of 21 Abraham Lincoln joined, and for the rest of his life was fixed to, the Northern party of business, called successively Federalist, Whig, Republican. It was the party opposed to Thomas Jefferson's small-government party of agriculture, called first, Republican, then Democrat. Agriculture and commerce are different and antagonistic, a conflict of interests demonstrated as far back as Greece and Rome. The urban commerce faction always defeats the country, farming party. The city has information, money, and organization not available in the country.

The antagonism between the two was recognized by Southern politicians who foresaw the coming tyranny of the larger and stronger money party. George Mason and Patrick Henry and others refused to sign the Constitution, begged the South not to ratify, and accurately forecasted what the North would do to them.

The central government was supported by a tax on imported goods, called tariff. The North lived by domestic industry, the South by export-import with Europe. The North did indeed attack the South by imposing its monetary policy on the South. To subsidize their industry the North began raising the tariff, blocking Southern trade with Europe. The South paid the taxes, the North spent the proceeds. That argument was over subsidizing the Northern merchant at the expense of the Southern farmer. There were no other conflicts except false ones.

The Northeastern money men (joined later by the Midwestern industrialists) were and are rich beyond the wildest imaginings of the ordinary citizen, especially the modest Southerner, who, having had to start from scratch in 1865, is still behind. The money men have been making money in a continuing addition for three hundred years: their carrying-trade monopoly, their slave trade's three-way passage, opium, manufacturing industry protected by government, subsidy called "internal improvements," control of banking and finance. They had enriched themselves from America's early wars while letting others do the fighting. They would add wealth from the next one, also from which they would subtract their bodies. They urged on the war but kept their distance from it, increasingly so thereafter.

It was that party of finance that Lincoln joined and remained ever their undeviating agent. He was the perfect party man, aggressively partisan. His party was the money party. He was a politician. He served the party.

The money party had lost the Executive Office to Thomas Jefferson in 1800, won it only a few times after, and then imperfectly. They became increasingly angry at the Democratic Party that had held the presidency so long. The money party did not lack power. The increasing Northern population majority gave them a continually increasing power in Congress. They had got much of what they wanted even with the opposite party in the presidency. That majority voted measures which subsidized Northern bankers, merchants, and manufacturers at the expense of Southern farmers. That party violated the Constitution and misinterpreted delegated powers, using government to subsidize Northern profits.

The South was abused. The tariff wounded the South's economy, injured its trade with Europe, protected and subsidized Northern industry. It excluded competition of European goods, forced the South to buy New England's goods, let New England manufacturers set their own prices. The tariff money paid by the South was received by the central government, and given to the North, in form of "internal improvements"—spending the money in North as businessmen directed. The South complained for fifty years, to no effect.

Territory—new states—was another disagreement. That one, too, was really money. The commerce party opposed admission of new states expected to be agricultural and vote against their monetary and mercantile preferment.

The sectional disagreement was entirely over money. The Northern money party had no valid argument for their un-Constitutional and selfish actions, so they threw into the forum the unrelated subject of slavery. It was the classical red herring, inserting into every disagreement a dishonest agitation to confuse understanding and divert attention from the real questions. The non-agricultural north had no use for slave labor so they sold their slaves over a period of 70 years.

The Northern money party agitated the hot, false "slavery issue" to give their cold, but real, war for power a moral cause. There are no moral wars. The North made war on the South to keep a captive market for their manufactures and a controlled source of cheap raw materials. That was Lincoln's party. It was a vehicle to power. No other American panted more after power or pursued it more doggedly than Abraham Lincoln. His mother and peers called him lazy: "He split fewer rails than any boy or man in the county." He was lazy, but "His ambition was an engine that never rested" (Herndon). His life "a breathless pursuit of office" (Lamon). Those closest to him said that he "had no business, no knowledge, no judgment. The only thing he knew was politics." He was an idler, not a worker, the classic "liberal." He had a selfish, cold, unsympathetic character. The kind of man capable of making a war.

Lincoln fought his way into Congress for one term. For his grandstanding his party would not renominate him. He retired in gloom. For five years he had no way to get notice. He considered himself politically dead. In 1854, the Democrats, having held the presidency for years, seemed to be again unstoppable with the popular Senator Douglas. Then Douglas had to write the bill to admit the territories of Kansas and Nebraska as states. Slavery was irrelevant to statehood but the Republicans falsely raised the "slavery issue." Without it there would have been quiet elections. The Democrats would have won."

The Republican Party did not love the slaves, they just hated the Democrats. They did not hate the institution of slavery, they loved "the issue" of slavery. If the Republicans had really cared for the welfare of the slaves, they would have done something for them, not something against others (and them). The condition of black people in the North was woeful. If their concern had been charitable they would not have been so hypocritical as to criminalize the South for an institution that had ended in the

North only a few years before. If he were sincere Lincoln would not have approved measures to exclude them from his state; he would not have excited Northern objection to black migration. He would not have waged war so viciously—on black and white. He would not have considered the slaves "contraband" so he could steal them for army labor gangs. The Republicans put the Negroes into an army too many Yankees did not want to join.

After the war, the Republicans had total power. If they had cared for the black people they would have hired them North instead of importing white labor. They would not have excluded them in their Homestead Act land donations. They would not have treated the Negroes so harshly in the North. They wanted the Negroes to stay South and vote Republican.

In 1856, levering himself to notice by agitating the "slavery issue," Lincoln became "a full time candidate for president." In 1858, he sent Herndon twelve hundred miles east to visit the money party politicians and pledge that he would do their bidding. In 1860, by using the Abolitionists' "slavery issue" the Republicans split the Democrats, at last seized the Executive Office, narrowly electing Abraham Lincoln as president. The politician gained power's highest reward. It was 60 years in the taking. The party would not give it up without a fight. The Republicans had the presidency and its rewards, but it was a weak hold.

Lincoln and his party were uneasy; he was not popular, neither were they. They had no firm constituency except Abolitionists, money men, and government-job seekers. Lincoln was viewed as a politician. There was a body of strong feeling against him in the North. That was apparent immediately after his election, after inauguration, and continually until the end of the war. Despite the severely-exercised power of war office—patronage, closing pulpits, imprisoning more than 35,000 people without charge, shutting down 300 opposition newspapers, despite Democrat departure and demoralization, the Democrats still managed to win many elections in the North. The Democrats gained much in 1862. Even in 1864, despite his managing the soldiers vote, jailing dissidents, intimidation by Republican mobs, stuffing ballot boxes, bringing in new partisan states, counting votes at bayonet point in New York City and other places, and with all Southern Democrats removed, his opponent won 84 votes for every 100 of Lincoln's. In 1864 the Northern vote against Lincoln was ten percent higher than in 1860. Lincoln never had full Northern support.

Peace is preferable to war for citizens, but not for politicians. Politicians like war. They are in politics for power; war confers the ultimate power. In this case it was even more desired. Even necessary. Peace would smother the infant Republican babe in its crib. Some Republicans, in the arrogance of finally beating the Democrats, publicly threatened war immediately after the election, even before South Carolina seceded. They were drunk with power. They knew they had the South and the Democratic Party at bay. But for how long?

The money party would lose life if the South were allowed out.

They had been talking for years about wanting to separate from the South because the South had been voting against their policy. Now that the South was out, the Northern money men took the opposite view. They realized they would lose the captive market for their manufactures, lose bank loans to the Southern farmers, lose a controlled source of cheap raw materials, lose the tariff subsidy, lose the benefit of interest on riskless tax-free government bonds based on increased public debt.

The Confederate States would be a low-tariff economy, next door to a high-tariff economy. Commerce would go South. Northern industrialists had no intention of submitting to such loss. The revenue that supported the central government and provided its surplus for spending was the tariff on foreign trade. The South, a fourth of the people, paid five-sixths of the taxes. The South paid for the central government which gave Southern earnings to the North.

If the South were allowed to leave the union, Northern industrialists would no longer be able to force the South through the tariff to buy Northern products. Europe's products would go to the South, escaping the North's world-high tariff. Charleston, Savannah, Mobile, and New Orleans would take Boston's commerce. It would not much affect the ordinary citizen of the North, but it would sorely grieve the money men. An independent

South would also deprive the party of their "moral issue." Opposition to "slavery" gave dignity to their party.

The Abolitionists were a strong, industrious part of the party. The money men and the Abolitionists needed each other. Take that issue away and the abolition movement would revert to a disdained few Jacobins, crackpots and revolutionaries. They were not harmless idealists, they were a party of Jacobins seeking power. Many were weird but they wanted to "rule the world." They would commit any violence upon society to gain and hold power. They were worse than the businessmen because they condemned private property, the foundation of stability and freedom.

The Abolitionists were valuable to the Republican Party. The two were fused, hard to separate. The Abolitionists were moneyed, the moneyed were Abolitionists. They were old Federalists-Whigs. Lincoln did what they told him. He never admitted to being part of either group. He ran away from public connection to the Abolitionists and talked "poor boy."

There was no national demand for war. Certainly the South did not want war. The South had no designs on the North. They just yearned to be left alone. They saw the signs: the Northern money party would stop at nothing. A cold war would become a hot one. Lincoln scoffed at such a fantasy while talking war in private. The South knew Lincoln better than the North did.

The Democratic Party did not want war. It was part of their platform that Lincoln's party threatened violent conflict ... The Democrats did not want the opposite party to gain possession of the power of war. The Northern people at large did not want war. Many Northern politicians said that if it was put to a vote, all the Northern states would have ratified any of the peace measures such as the Crittenden Compromise. Lincoln received thousands of Northern entreaties to maintain peace. Many Republican politicians and voters did not want war. They still put peace before party, instinctively believed that war was unthinkable. It was the old universal story—the people want peace, the elite want war.

Most Americans wanted peace. There was no national movement, no mood, for war.

Even Lincoln's cabinet, at first, did not want war. But the faction to whom Lincoln listened did want war. General Halleck later said, "The Radicals had his ear; he always ended up doing what they asked." The radicals welcomed war. If he did not give them a war they would make war on him. It would have taken considerable courage for him to oppose his core backers. Why should he, he had been one with them his entire political life.

It can be said with certainly: the immediate cause of the war was the politicians wanting "power, plunder, and extended rule." If that was not their goal they would not have needed war. At first, a good number of Northern businessmen, even some in New England, did not want war. That is to their credit. It is not to their credit that once Lincoln started it they joined him with alacrity. They quickly saw the reward-risk ratio of joining versus opposing him. Better rule than ruin. Lincoln's party had been making war on the South for generations. Their belligerence was not a sudden impulse.

Whether the economic war would become a shooting war was in the hands of Lincoln.

If he had allowed peace, the American people, each individual person, afflicted enough with life's inherent personal troubles, could have gone about their business, doing the best they could to find some happiness, not always successful, but at least unwounded by war, uninjured, unmolested by a man they had never seen. And who had never seen them.

Even with the aids of the electorate confused by the slavery agitation and the Democrats knifing each other, the people had only given him 39% of the vote. Unless the North was rallied by war, there was every chance the Democrats could drive the Republicans out of power. Ever since he was elected, the Republicans had been lining up demanding their share of the rewards of patronage. Their message was simple: we got you elected, now you pay off. They knew and he knew that if their party lost power, they would all lose their plums. Lincoln knew he needed them and they knew they needed him. Lincoln had thousands of offices to distribute to those who had worked to elect him.

Lincoln's Springfield associates described him as cold, selfish, hypersensitive to his own ills, indifferent to the condition of others except to resent their successes. That he cared naught for the horrors of war is clear. In 1859 he predicted to Herndon war and the need of finding a man strong enough to win it. Even before his inauguration he privately spoke his war plans to Salmon Chase, Herndon, and Lyman Trumbull: "I'll make a cemetery of the South." The same promise the French Jacobins made of the farmers in 1790. He did not worry over starting a war; his closest associates said that as president he never worried over the suffering caused by his war—he said, "I sleep good and enjoy my rations."

Lincoln's fellows said he was a "most close-mouthed, reticent, cunning politician." (Herndon, Lamon, Stewart, Trumbull, Seward.) He was careful what he said even to intimates. But clearly he did not worry over war's evils. Lincoln consummately practiced the art of deception, making every audience, public or private, infer what he wanted them to believe. He told those who worried over the possibility of war that he opposed war. Most of the American people opposed it, the South dreaded it. It is certain that Lincoln did not dread the horror of war, his only concern was that the Northern people might not accept his war or that his war might fail. He said enough to show he did not worry over what he did, only over defeat. He did not fear war, was cynically indifferent to the superiority of peace.

"Cold, uncaring of the needs of others, self-loving." That is what Lincoln's Springfield lawyer associates said of him. A man like that is the kind of man who could not comprehend the ill of war, would not care if he could. The kind of man who could start a war.

Power ambition is the only way to explain Lincoln's and his party's conduct; there is no other way. Later on, in 1867, they would savagely attack the hapless Andrew Johnson. They could no longer hide simple power lust by the "slavery issue." Johnson, at first disliked by the South, then disliked by the North, had the courage to stand up to the vicious Radicals after the war. Many have claimed that Lincoln would have done the same. He could not stand up to them before the war and would not have stood up after it. That contrast between Johnson and Lincoln, observed by their peers, does tell something of Lincoln's character.

Without war the country would rest safe, his party would convulse and die. The moneyed men and Abolitionists—his core support—would react in fury and throw him away in disgrace. An independent South would deprive the moneyed of their money and the Abolitionists of their issue. War not merely saved his party—it would raise its backers to wealth and power America had never seen.

It would, of course, kill some people. No matter.

Why war? Not to abolish slavery. That subject had been agitated as a means to win election, to divide the Democrats, polarize the country, and frighten the Northern people with a "peril." Lincoln elected, that issue was of no more use. Lincoln not only said so, he acted on it—he promised every protection of slavery. Not a word said of starting a war against slavery.

For politicians the most important consideration is to keep office. They know better than the citizens that they are in office to get money and power. Their backers do not love them, they support them for self-interest. To stay in power strong measures were required. The easiest way to gain power is to usurp it—take it, if you can. War seemed the solution.

Lincoln and history have succeeded in hiding it, but Lincoln's only solid support was the Radical Republicans. They were his sponsors and directors. Except for them there was no desire for war in the North, even among the Republican voters, and the total Republican vote was only 39%. Not long before the war Jefferson Davis had been warmly received even in New England. Benjamin Butler, who joined Lincoln later and became one of his most vicious agents when it served his interest, was most hospitable to Davis. Many people in the North thought the South had justice and right, even provocation, on their side.

After the war Confederate General James Longstreet joined the Republican Party at the request of his old friend, General-President Grant. Longstreet had helped Grant financially when they were young, introduced Grant to his cousin Julia, helped him to win her despite Grant's handicaps. It is presumed Grant was grateful because he loved Julia. After the war the South was suffering under a second Northern attack—"Reconstruction." Grant told Longstreet that Southerners ought to leave the Democratic Party and join the Republican. Then they could be rid of abuse and gain patronage, suggesting that the whole conflict had been but a fight over political power and its rewards.

On March 2, 1861, the U.S. Congress set the highest tariff ever, on iron goods almost 60%. On 11 March, the Confederate Congress set tariffs at 5-10%. The Northern businessmen, Republican and Democrat, reacted in fury. August Belmont, Rothschild agent in the United States, a Democrat, changed from promoting peace to war. Northern money men and Northern politicians descended on Lincoln. He had always done what the money men asked. This time they wanted war. He gave them war.

Who started the War to Prevent Southern Independence? Who bears that shame? The Republican Party elite wanted it. Much of the responsibility belongs to the party politicians and Northern money men—merchants, bankers, manufacturers. They wanted war, they commanded Lincoln to make it, but they could not command the army. Only Lincoln had the power to write the order. He did that by himself. In few wars can one man be so solely incriminated. If he had said, "No," there would have been no war.

Presidents Buchanan, Pierce, and Fillmore, all Northerners but not anti-South, have been portrayed as inferior to Lincoln. They did not make war on their people or the Constitution. Pierce was derided by Lincoln but admired by Hawthorne. Who is the better judge, the politician or the Christian? All three are today nearly unknown. Is anonymity the mark of Cain? Or is murder? Is a man who makes war to escape anonymity superior to a man who will not? Those unknowns were far better than Lincoln. Is it possible to be esteemed, to rise to the heights of public admiration for taking the opposite course, killing all those people, destroying property, single-handedly making a violent revolution that transforms a republic into an empire? Is it better to make war than to make peace?

Lincoln was not a peaceable man forced into war. Herndon related a conversation that took place "one morning in 1859." Lincoln said, "The advocates of State Sovereignty always remind me of the fellow who contended that the proper place for the big kettle was inside the little one." That silliness is a typical specimen of Lincoln "wit"—unoriginal, borrowed, trite, meaningless, applied to any subject whether related or not, a dishonest evasion of the question, everything reduced to a slogan. Worse, it makes clear his enmity to the federal system, without which there is no freedom. Lincoln's method always was to obscure thought by introducing an unrelated anecdote, whose real effect was to mask the subject, or change the subject.

He and Herndon discussed war between the sections. Both thought it was all right, neither evinced any worry of its horror. Herndon raised the question of Northern agreement to war: "I feared the North would have difficulty controlling the various classes of people and shades of sentiment, so as to make them an effective force for war." Lincoln told him not to worry. "If war is inevitable, one big man, greater than the rest, will leap forth armed and equipped—the people's leader in the conflict." Lincoln wanted to be the "big man."

Abraham Lincoln made a war to prevent Southern independence. The war was not necessary. Peace would prosper his country, peace would preserve the lives of his people. War would prosper his party, and kill his people. It was Lincoln's war, just another form of what he had been doing all his life. The war was conceived, planned, actuated, prosecuted, and perfected, as no more than another political exercise. He was incapable of seeing it, or anything else, in any other way.

In the last week of the war, after Lee had evacuated Richmond and Petersburg, Lincoln visited those towns. He was eager to visit the White House of the Confederacy, pleased to sit in Jefferson Davis's chair. He sat so long, reveling in the symbol of his seat, that his officers uneasily reminded him that it was time to move on to other calls. Walking about the streets, he was astonished that not a single white person appeared to greet him. That the populace remained behind closed doors, not even looking from the windows, was real evidence, not symbolic as was his taking possession of the deposed president's chair. Their conduct was proof of loyalty to their cause.

That kind of loyalty would not have been his in Washington City if he had lost. Lincoln had started his war by demand of a PARTY ELITE; it was not the people who wanted it. He had thought there must be in the South, as there was in the North, a large body of opposition to their government. That none came to greet him, even when their cause was dead, their condition desperate, totally in the power of their enemy, shows a truth. Davis defeated had more sincere love than Lincoln victorious. The South, in defeat, gave more devotion to its cause than the North gave to his power. Returning to Washington City, he told the South-hating Senator Sumner that whites would have to be disfranchised and Negroes franchised, otherwise Democrats would regain control of the government and the Republicans would be right back where they were before the war.

That the war was of Lincoln's own making was a fact known to much of the North and Europe, and all the South. But not to posterity. Victory writes history. To justify the outrage of Lincoln's useless war requires excluding facts, twisting truth, making fantasy. Of that war the facts are clear, the events are conclusive. It is foolish to say that human beings make a war and wage it so viciously for charity. The motive was power lust, the worst of sins, the Devil's Proposition. Mankind are willing and able to see base motives of their acquaintances, people nearby. But they ennoble the motives of their powerful rulers, proportional to their power and proportional to their distance from them. Especially dead ones, and more so if they are "martyred."

While living Lincoln was not much esteemed. Then a gunshot made him a "martyr." Public opinion swung to adulation. Adulation of a man who never lived. And of a cause that never existed. Would Lincoln, if the Devil gave him the choice, have chosen death in order to triumph over anonymity? Would he have been willing to die to be remembered? That he was killed was not good for Lincoln's body, but it was good for his image. Dying relieved him of blame, even sanctified his name. Living, he would have had to live with his work in the results of his war. Shorn of war's protecting armor his naked politics could not be hid. He could not have escaped much blame.

Lincoln knew how to initiate a war. He had no idea of the magnitude, the horror, and the consequences of his actions. His friends said he was not a deep thinker. A politician, his mind never went any further than politics. He was capable of no more. He was one of the most political animals who ever polluted American air. Maybe the chief of the chiefs considering the damage done. He acted from strictly political motives and had not considered the cost in material and human ruin.

He did not worry over the war. In April 1865, at City Point in the heart of devastated Virginia, saluted by a vast army, he and Sumner, exultant, reveling in their power, could not resist joining arms in a little dance. He was unconcerned, even glad, that he had destroyed his own federal republic and not ashamed that he had replaced it with an imperial despotism—that he ruled. The suggestion that he made war for principle is absurd.

He did get just what he wanted. More than any other American, he got fame, the terrestrial immortality that would make him remembered as long as America lives. His fame, his adulation, is entirely the consequence of war. He did not care for the war's other consequences, but he knew that one.

Wars are made for gain, not for God. Why should a man who spent his life pursuing power be praised? Why should Abraham Lincoln, the Godless man, be made a god? Why should a man who rejected Christ, who pursued the Devil's Proposition with a "breathless anxiety," be labeled a Christ-like character? Even more astounding, he was bestowed that honor for one single horrible deed, the most horrible action a man can take—making a war. He had lived fifty-two years without his associates considering him exceptional, thought of as a self-centered man, a cunning politician and no more. Without the war he would have lived and died as other men—unknown and forgotten. Lincoln is responsible for making the war and then waging it viciously against his own people. Counting civilians, he killed a million people. And killed his own country.

Posterity has conferred upon Lincoln fame. What he deserves is shame, shame as great as any tyrant who ever applied the rod. History, failing its duty, has accepted the image he and his party fashioned. History has closed its eyes to the obvious character of the man, to human nature, to the real way human affairs are conducted. Reality broadcasts that he coolly planned, contrived, commenced, and directed a program for usurpation. Nobody listens.

War is the worst of human horrors; Lincoln's war was America's worst. History says he made war in pursuit of "Union," a supposedly good thing, a word that is not required to mean anything—an end in itself.

Later on, the false claim was added that he fought to eradicate slavery. Union, at the point of a gun, is slavery. Private slavery is Heaven compared to the government slavery he fastened on his country.

Lincoln's wonderful act of mercy was the only case in the world where that worldwide system of labor was ended by war. The supposed benefactors of his war were the worst hurt. Grievously hurt during the war, their misery was prolonged for years after the war. As a compassionate and practical matter, the war did not justify wreaking so much suffering upon slaves and ex-slaves, so injuring the economy on which their livelihood depended it took four score years to recover. It has been estimated that a fourth of the black population perished during the war. Both races suffered and epidemic of death and morbidity.

Why war? Who emerged from it better off? Did it help anybody to destroy so much property? Did it help the million who were killed, the millions who were wounded, their families, the many millions ruined? Did it help the Southern soldiers and civilians, black and white, who died? Did it help the slaves to be freed into a land so deprived of wealth that they starved? Did Lincoln's war help the dead and maimed Yankee soldiers? The ordinary Northern citizen?

Did it help anybody but government officers and war profiteers?

How about the awful moral damage of war? Was the ensuing "Gilded Age" good? Lincoln changed the government of the people from republic to empire. Was that improvement? Is empire better than republic?

The Swiss painter Frank Buscher lived in Washington for several years. He called the Republican leaders "the most contemptible human beings I have ever known." After the war he met Lee, painted his portrait, saw him every day for six weeks, and for the rest of his life referred to him as "that great man."

It is undisputed fact that wars are made for power. The very life of Abraham Lincoln, his every word and deed, can be explained only as a single-minded pursuit of power. He did nothing to indicate that he ever thought on a higher level. He has been elevated to a dignity he did not deserve because he made a big ugly war and spoke some pretty little words. Literary criticism has failed its duty. Pretty phrases gathered over a lifetime and sprinkled, sometimes inappropriately, into speeches, do not mean truth or make right. His words were shallow and pretty, his works deep and ugly.

Of America's paramount event, the paramount question is: Why? Why was there a war between the once-united states in America? Because one man made a war. All he had to do not to have a war was just not make it.

Why War? Two men of the highest possible authority supply the answer: The first said, "there are always men springing up who are so full of pride and ambition, so thirsty for distinction, so hungry for power and glory that they will stop at nothing, whether it means building an empire or tearing one down, whether at the expense of emancipating slaves, or enslaving free men." That was said by Abraham Lincoln in 1838.

The second authority spoke in 1869. He was asked, "Was the war necessary? What was the cause of the war, why was it fought?" He answered, "War was by no means necessary; it could easily have been avoided. The war was made by the possessors of the Federal Executive. They wanted to gain control of the country, and to obtain that control would shrink back at nothing. Even greater cost than it did would not have mattered to them. No matter how great the damage, those men would do it again." That is the war as given by Robert E. Lee.

Abraham Lincoln is allowed to get away with his cant: "And the war came." The war did not "come"—Abraham Lincoln brought it. The mistaken belief that slavery had something to do with the war has confused understanding. If there had never been one slave in the United States the money men would still have done anything necessary to obtain their government-sponsored profits, including making war.

Why war? Because the wrong man sat in the president's chair. Why did Abraham Lincoln choose war? Because he did not fear God.

Lessons of the War to Prevent Southern Independence

THE SECOND ATTEMPT OF AMERICAN states to gain independence failed of success. Not from weak principle, or weak character of the people. Preventing their success required all the force a political party, controlling a powerful government, could command: waging America's bloodiest war by a policy deliberately savage and cruel.

The independence attempt failed. But it succeeded exquisitely in defining the nation. And gloriously in defining freedom. It is impossible to comprehend the United States of America without studying that struggle. The Southern Independence War describes and displays the United States of America. It reveals what that nation was meant to be, it determined what it has become.

The war was fought for one reason, and that gives it its only correct name: "The War to Prevent Southern Independence."

For four years Abraham Lincoln executed a military tyranny at home and waged a war by a new policy that violated practice and compacts signed by civilized countries. He killed a million people.

He made a revolution: he changed the form of America's government from republic to empire. He made a government of consolidated power. He killed a government of the people by the people, of limited and local power. He killed self-determination, government by consent of the governed. Power can be limited only by some form of opposing power. Because Abraham Lincoln destroyed state power, there remains no way to prevent the central government from defining its own power. Abraham Lincoln made a system wherein the government can take all power.

He destroyed the federal system. He won his war. His supporters write the history.

The second attempt by its states for independence is the backbone of America's history and essence of its character. That story must be understood to understand America. It tells how the American states designed a government, how they meant to be governed, how they were governed for a while, what became of that system, and why.

There is no way to explain Abraham Lincoln's conduct except by the logical and obvious reason that underlies all wars—pursuit of power: The Devil's Proposition.

Abraham Lincoln was guilty of treason:

1. He made a dishonest tumult to gain power. He betrayed his country with the false issue of "the expansion of slavery."

2. He made a war, to usurp power.

3. He conducted his war by savage method: evil and cruel. Europeans and United States had agreed to international rule of war conduct, that women, children, non-combatant land, and property were to be spared. Recent wars had been fought between armies on fields separate from habitations, the fighting limited to armies only. He departed from that rule. The most vicious of his generals were those he sponsored—Pope, Hunter, Butler, Sherman, and Sheridan. His army destroyed property, stole property, his generals stole property. He waged war upon women and children. General Sherman admitted that only 20% of his destruction had any military value, the rest was wanton. Lincoln made war on his own people.

4. He violated the Constitution egregiously and repeatedly.

5. He destroyed his government, the republic and forced into its place an empire. He inherited a confederacy, a union of sovereign states, and a government of limited and diffused power, a government by the people. He destroyed it and

put in its place a consolidated government with all power concentrated in the head.

One man can change history. Solely by himself, one man changed the government of America from a confederacy to an empire. One man got us in the Southern War. Subsequently one man got us in World War I. One man got us in World War II. We gained nothing from those wars. We lost much.

The lovable and wonderful Samuel Johnson (1709-1784) said that the acts of rulers, good or bad, have little to do with the happiness of each individual, that it is personal events, not government acts, which determine happiness. Johnson's statement needs to be read by those who believe in government, in socialist progress, in change, improvement—the people who call themselves "liberals," progressives, modernists. They are all really Jacobins, but ashamed to admit it.

In Johnson's day people lived under weak governments, in small states whose rulers had little power. They even fought their wars on limited terms, leaving non-combatants out of it. Then the "liberals" (Jacobins) took charge. Lincoln was the first American "liberal." "Liberals" have controlled our world since because of the revolution he wrought. They have wrenched power away from the private citizen and localities and conferred that power upon formerly-weak central governments. They made big government. They brought world wars that could not have occurred without big government; they brought class hatred, domestic crime and public disorder, death to hundreds of millions. All due to "liberals" and their big government.

Those who believe the world is better can look at the violent era birthed by Abraham Lincoln. Rulers have caused more misery since big government came than personal afflictions and natural disasters combined. Men are little, but an ant commanding an elephant can pull down the tent. And the temple.

Some way must be found to protect us from the weakness and folly of one man. By himself, one man can do only limited damage; but commanding the power of a strong government he can do almost unlimited injury. For millions he can destroy everything they possess.

What did Lincoln and his war accomplish? He made one of our worst ecological disasters. He permanently distorted race relations. He killed morals, more so in victorious North than in the defeated South. He killed more Americans than all the other wars combined. He rooted up the fragile flower of federalism and planted in its place the rampant rod of empire. That usurpation made the pattern for the big government and their big wars that have never stopped since. He put the state in the place of God.

When Lincoln left the stage, he left the South in a cage and the North in a rage. That other actor—what was his name?—did less damage.

To esteem Abraham Lincoln is to respect words more than deeds. Those who live by the pen envy their colleague who rose to the greater glory of the sword.

Once upon a time people had no house key, never took their car key out of the switch; now they lock both while they are inside them. Our government officers, pandering to the vicious, have destroyed law and order, made the citizens victims of domestic criminals. Pandering to foreign factions they have made most of the world hate us. The ruling class orders us to empty our treasury and kill our boys making war halfway around the world on countries who pose no threat to us. People say the spirit of love that once reigned here has been replaced by hate: God replaced by government.

If enough people would learn how government really operates, so that history's lesson could be learned and applied, then, finally, at last, man's long, gloomy story could begin to brighten.

Don't look for it to happen. The Jacobins are in control. They have the power and they will not give it up unless forced. They own the government—the decision and the enforcement. They determine public opinion through government control and private ownership of the opinion institutions. They control the man who controls the army. They control the academy. "*Veritas*" is inscribed on university seals, not in university policy.

The vast American economy is dominated by a faction and that faction commands a government of unlimited power. America is governed by a plutocracy—an oligarchy of several hundred millionaires. International money men. They have the kingdom and the power. It is easy for them to find, or if necessary to make, a public figure who wants the glory. They will direct him. The condition of the United States Government in the 21st century A.D. makes that clear. The combination of private money and government power is called fascism.

Abraham Lincoln wanted the glory. There are plenty of Lincolns around today. Whether the power is controlled by one, few, or many, there will always be a surplus of rulers who will do the bidding of whoever is in charge. For the Kingdom, the Power, and the Glory they will burn another country, or their own, to boil their breakfast eggs.

Man forgets that the Kingdom, the Power, and the Glory belong not to man, but to God.

There is a first step that must be taken before we can hope for true freedom. Admit the truth. Tell the truth. Jefferson Davis was right. In the dying days of the Confederacy, Davis said,

"There is another reason we must continue the struggle. If we are defeated, we shall be forced to drink the last bitter dregs of our cup of humiliation and see the story of our cause written by the New England Historians."

Read the biographies of John C. Calhoun. You will see a man of integrity. Read about Lincoln as described by those closest to him—Herndon, "Herndon's Informants," and Lamon. You will see a politician. One struggling for principle, the other fighting for place.

The truth of the Confederate strife, the truth of all strife, has not yet been received. It is not perceived, it is not even presented. Never in America's history has truth been so buried and distorted.

It is under that burden that all Americans labor in their quest for freedom.

Let the truth be told.

Sources

TO UNDERSTAND ABRAHAM LINCOLN ONE must study not his words, but the words of William H. Herndon, closest to him in Springfield, and of Ward Hill Lamon, closest to him in Washington. His words were cant, their words were candid. Herndon knew Lincoln for 31 years, slept in same room with him for four years, worked in same room with him 18 years, and was political confidante and consultant for twenty-five. Lamon was a close enough law partner that Lincoln kept him at his side when he left Springfield, put him next door in the White House. Lamon saw him every day for four years.

Herndon, nine years younger, and Lamon, nineteen years younger than Lincoln, esteemed their chief. Their chief esteemed himself, condescended to both of them. They called him "Mr. Lincoln," he called them "Billy" and "Hill." Living as a part of his supreme national power, it is natural that they would be partisan; what is a remarkable tribute to their integrity is their candor. Most men would have succumbed to the advantages of sanctifying his eminence. Herndon and Lamon admitted to curtailing their revelations. For revealing what truths they did, they suffered obloquy the rest of their lives.

Lamon's first book is out of print. Reading his long chapter on Lincoln's character one can understand why Lincoln lovers lambaste Lamon. His analysis is consonant with Herndon's, and confirmed by the opinions of Lincoln's peers. Herndon knew Lincoln; he was a regular Boswell in searching out what others knew, in writing it down, in telling the truth. Without Herndon, Lincoln would be a god indeed. Without Herndon there would be no possibility of history ever coming close to the real Lincoln. Except perhaps in the far distant future, when posterity might at last concede that the man's deeds prove his character.

Herndon was Lincoln's admirer, lackey, researcher, philosophical link to the Abolitionists, and political link to the Eastern Republicans. Herndon's connections and work were of exceeding value to Lincoln. Without Herndon, Lincoln's grasp might have fallen short of his reach. For a quarter of a century Herndon subordinated himself to his selfish, single-minded partner and operated the law office while Lincoln politicked outside. He conducted Lincoln's business, ran Lincoln's errands, supplied information and furnished connections to the centers of Republican power. Herndon was an intellectual, Lincoln was shallow. Herndon gave the thought, Lincoln the talk. Herndon made the foundation for Lincoln's platform.

Herndon was an Abolitionist, not a bully, milder than the New England variety. A few Abolitionists were sincere zealots, most were non-demented power seekers. They were not idealists, but pursuers of the Devil's Proposition, taking advantage of the good will of the ordinary decent citizens in order to use them. That identity has been lost, most observers still consider them idealists. A few have seen the truth, Hawthorne for one. He had the intelligence to see it, and the courage to say it, when it was dangerous. It is easier to see nowadays, but come to think of it, it is still dangerous to say it.

Herndon called himself "an extreme Radical." He was a sincere leftist, guided Lincoln, and rejoiced in Lincoln's revolution. John Randolph of Roanoke said, "All radicals are either fools or knaves."

Herndon the fool, Lincoln the knave. Herndon really believed the pernicious notions of the Enlightenment. In France such belief led to Robespierre, Revolution, killing, and destruction of a nation. In America it led to Lincoln, Revolution, killing, and destruction of two nations. Herndon proudly declared himself radical. Lincoln had not the brain to understand, the sympathy to care, or the candor to declare, but he did have the will to use the Jacobin ambition to execute and political sense to hide, their programs of man replacing God. Herndon thought Lincoln's revolution would save the world.

On December 20, 1890, Herndon wrote a letter to Truman Bartlett. By then, Lincoln had been dead the same number of years that Herndon had lived with him. Herndon had shed his radical belief. He had long ago rejected the very essence of Lincoln's party—tariff protection of Northern finance (the cause of the Northern War to Prevent Southern Independence) He had lost affection for leftist revolution. He wrote: "The old strivers for power are replaced by new ones: the Knights of Labor, the Farmers' Alliance, the Woman's Temperance Union swallowing up the Woman's Rights Party, the splits in the women's movements. The reformers can't somehow agree and stick. The idea of the single tax is growing and so is communism, anarchism. Other wild isms are struggling. The devil seems to be on hand everywhere."

As the years lengthened, Herndon's musings came to show less and less faith in man, and more in God. William H. Herndon died March 1, 1891.

Much of Herndon is given in *Herndon's Informants* by Douglas L. Wilson and Rodney O. Davis. One cannot adequately thank Dr. Wilson and Dr. Davis for editing Herndon's information and adding much to it. Their book, Herndon's, and Lamon's give any person of sense a clear idea regarding the real Abraham Lincoln. He was an ordinary, weak mortal, with an extraordinary desire to become strong.

Roy P. Basler, *Collected Works of Abraham Lincoln*, 1953

James C. Bonner, ed., *Plantation Experiences of a New York Woman*, Greene County Public Library, Snow Hill, NC, 1956

Frank Buscher, *Mein Leben and Streben in Amerika*, Leipzig, 1942

Congressional Globe, 38th Cong., 1st Sess.

Samuel W. Crawford, *The Genesis of the Civil War, The Story of Sumter, 1860-1861*, 1887

David H. Donald, *Lincoln's Herndon*, 1948

Will Durant, letter to author

David Hackett Fischer, *Albion's Seed: Four British Folkways in America*, 1989

Robert W. Fogel and Stanley L. Engerman, *Time on the Cross: The Economics of American Negro Slavery*, 1974

William Henry Herndon, *Herndon's Lincoln: The True Story of a Great Life*, 1889

Emanuel Herz, *The Hidden Lincoln: From the Letters and Papers of William H. Herndon*, 1940

Ward Hill Lamon, *The Life of Abraham Lincoln*, 1872

_____, *Recollections of Abraham Lincoln, 1847-1865*, 1895

Alexander K. McClure, *Abraham Lincoln and Men of War-Times*, 1996

Edgar Lee Masters, *Lincoln - The Man*, 1931

New-York Historical Society, *The Confidential Correspondence of Gustavus Vasa Fox*, 1918-1919

John G. Nicolay and John Hay, *Abraham Lincoln*, 1890

Northampton County, Virginia, Court Records

Stephen B. Oates, *With Malice Toward None: The Life of Abraham Lincoln*, 1977

Official Records of the War of the Rebellion, 1880-1901

Theodore C. Pease and James G. Randall, eds., *The Diary of Orville H. Browning, 1850-1891*

Charles W. Ramsdell, "Lincoln and Fort Sumter," *Journal of Southern History*, vol. 3, 1937

_____, "The Natural Limits of Slavery Expansion," *Mississippi Valley Historical Review*, vol. 16, 1929

Anne E. Rowe, *The Enchanted Country: Northern Writers in the South, 1865-1910*, 1978

Raphael Semmes, *Memoirs of Service Afloat, During the War Between the States*, 1868

Kenneth Shorey, ed., *Letters of John Randolph of Roanoke to Dr. John Brockenbrough,* 1812-1833, 1988

Pleasant A. Stovall, *Robert Toombs, Statesman…*, 1892

John S. Tilley, *Lincoln Takes Command*, 1941

Alexis de Tocqueville, *Democracy in America*, 1848

Frank van der Linden, *Lincoln: The Road to War,* 1998

Henry C. Whitney, *Life on the Circuit with Abraham Lincoln*, 1892

_____, *Lincoln the Citizen*, 1907

Douglas L. Wilson and Rodney O. Davis, eds., *Herndon's Informants*, 1998

Edmund Wilson, *Patriotic Gore: Studies in the Literature of the American Civil War*, 1962

Available From Shotwell Publishing

IF YOU ENJOYED THIS BOOK, perhaps some of our other titles will pique your interest. The following titles are currently available from Shotwell at all major online book retailers.

A Legion of Devils: Sherman in South Carolina by Karen Stokes

Annals of the Stupid Party: Republicans Before Trump by Clyde N. Wilson

Carolina Love Letters by Karen Stokes

Confederaphobia: An American Epidemic by Paul C. Graham

Dismantling the Republic by Jerry C. Brewer

Dixie Rising: Rules for Rebels by James R. Kennedy

Emancipation Hell: The Tragedy Wrought By Lincoln's Emancipation Proclamation by Kirkpatrick Sale

Lies My Teacher Told Me: The True History of the War for Southern Independence by Clyde N. Wilson

Maryland, My Maryland: The Cultural Cleansing of a Small Southern State by Joyce Bennett.

Nullification: Reclaiming Consent of the Governed by Clyde N. Wilson

Punished with Poverty: The Suffering South by James R. & Walter D. Kennedy

Segregation: Federal Policy or Racism? by John Chodes

Southern Independence. Why War?- The War to Prevent Southern Independence by Dr. Charles T. Pace

Southerner, Take Your Stand! by John Vinson

Washington's KKK: The Union League During Southern Reconstruction by John Chodes.

When the Yankees Come: Former South Carolina Slaves Remember Sherman's Invasion. Edited with Introduction by Paul C. Graham

The Yankee Problem: An American Dilemma by Clyde N. Wilson

GREEN ALTAR BOOKS (Literary Imprint)

A New England Romance & Other SOUTHERN Stories by Randall Ivey

Tiller by James Everett Kibler

GOLD-BUG MYSTERIES (Mystery & Suspense Imprint)

To Jekyll and Hide by Martin L. Wilson

SHOTWELL
COLUMBIA
SO. CAR.
EST. 2015
PUBLISHING

Made in the USA
Middletown, DE
24 August 2024